Beyond the Barriers

HULL LEGACY SERIES

Sponsored by the
Mountain Brook Baptist Church
Birmingham, Alabama

1. *Harbingers of Hope: Claiming God's Promises in Today's World*, 2007.
2. *Seminary in Crisis: The Strategic Response of The Southern Baptist Theological Seminary to the SBC Controversy*, 2010.

3. *Beyond the Barriers: Overcoming Hostility in the Church*, Revised Edition, 2012.

William E. Hull is Research Professor, Samford University, and Theologian in Residence, Mountain Brook Baptist Church, both in Birmingham, Alabama.

Beyond the Barriers

Overcoming Hostility In The Church

Revised Edition

William Edward Hull

Hull Legacy Series, Volume III
Mountain Brook Baptist Church
Birmingham, Alabama

Samford University Press
Birmingham, Alabama

Mercer University Press
Macon, Georgia

MUP/H848
©2012 Mercer University Press
1400 Coleman Avenue
Macon, Georgia 31207 USA

Printed in the United States of America

Unless otherwise noted, scripture quotations are from the Revised Standard Version of the Bible (RSV), 2nd ed. (c1971, 1977 by the Division of Christian Education of the National Council of the Churches of Christ in the U.S.A.) and are used by permission. Quotation of other ancient sources, such as Josephus, are from the Loeb Classical Library except when another translation is cited in the notes.

Revised edition. First edition published by Broadman Prress (c1981); copyright assigned to William E. Hull, 2007.

Books published by Mercer University Press are printed on acid-free paper that meets the requirements of American National Standard for Information Sciences—Permanence of Paper for Printed Library Materials.

Mercer University Press is a member of Green Press Initiative <greenpressinitiative.org>, a nonprofit organization working to help publishers and printers increase their use of recycled papers and decrease their use of fiber derived from endangered forests.

Library of Congress Cataloging-in-Publication Data

Hull, William Edward, 19xx—
Beyond the Barriers : Overcoming Hostility in the Church
Revised edition.
pp. cm.
Includes bibliographical references.
ISBN 978-0-88146-xxx-x (hardcover : acid-free paper)
1. Hull, William E. (William Edward) 19xx--. 2.

Contents

MERCER
UNIVERSITY PRESS

Endowed by
Tom Watson Brown
and
The Watson-Brown Foundation, Inc.

Foreword

Rising early, my father wheels to his desk to begin work before breakfast. For months, he has steeped himself in the history of the Berlin Wall; thick books are veined with his red pen, tracing the Wall's surprise overnight rise, its 28-mile outrage severing the lifeblood of a city, and its equally staggering fall. He once lived in close proximity to that border, and later, when the wall still knifed its way through the heart of a common people, he wrote a book wound around that image calling church and society to dismantle the strongholds that divide us by race, religion, sex, social class.

Now, thirty years later, *Beyond the Barriers* is being reprinted; and he is churning through major revisions. He is making his way through the fallen stones to touch the scar on the landscape, to feel what barbed wires still remain, constrain, and wrongly invade our Wholeness. His weakened hand presses pen to paper the old-fashioned way, slowly, slowly, but with a fierce force of will. He is devoted with the full length of his life to reconciliation. To the Oneness we are and can yet be.

There is urgency in his hand, for he is living in close proximity, now, to another wall–the one between the living and the dead. Our cultural mind can no longer imagine this, as perhaps people once did—a permeable boundary. We have failed to imagine it natural, or graceful, to cross over, trusting the hospitality of the other side. Death's realm is severed from us, a fortress surrounds it; and we rarely speak of it, though it cuts through the heart of everything.

Even this week, as a wall is going up in my garden—a strong, tall stroke of definition; my father is leveling his own final barrier to Wholeness. In the mysterious world of amyotrophic lateral sclerosis ("Lou Gehrig's disease," ALS), one is allotted time, mercifully or not, to approach the perimeter between life and death, to peer over, to become acquainted, as it were, with the other side–not as an enemy to oppose but as a mystery to enter. One is asked, with each muscle lost, each word eroded, each freedom clipped, to put down that particular stone. One by one. To dismantle one's life; slowly dismantle one's life, and walk knowingly into what is beyond.

One day, my father will be on the other side of this dividing wall, while I yet grope toward it, darkly. I want to believe it is not as impenetrable as we think, this wall between us. That even across this great divide, we are somehow yet joined in a mystery I dare not name.

There is a place, as the 13th-century Persian mystic Rumi says, out there beyond right and wrong, beyond male and female, black and white, even; and I want to add, beyond the living and the dead. There is a field with no walls at all, where all is one, and reconciled. To my father, I want to say now, I want to say in all the years to come:

I'll meet you there.
I'll meet you there.
—*Susan Hull Walker*

(From my daughter's blog, "A Still Life . . . A Life Still"
http://alifestill.com)

Dedicated
to

the Members of
Mountain Brook Baptist Church
Birmingham, Alabama

and to its

Senior Minister
(1981--2011)
James D. Moebes

Partners in ministry
1991--2011

Preface

In 1981 I published *Beyond the Barriers* that offered a study of reconciliation for the contemporary church. The content of that volume was hammered out in a series of sermons and teaching sessions shortly after I became pastor of the First Baptist Church in Shreveport, Louisiana, and sought to address some of its most pressing needs. Here was a congregation typical of almost all Southern Baptist churches in the Deep South at that time. Its membership was limited to Anglo-Saxons, its leadership to middle-age and older males. Laity was so deferential to clergy that the members did not see themselves as ministers but only as facilitators of whatever the pastor might ask them to do. Without realizing it or fully intending it, here was a church full of walls that not only shut out many whom they should have been reaching but also segregated themselves into traditional groupings that limited their usefulness.

Fortunately, by the time that the book was published six years into my ministry there, the church had responded positively to the preaching and teaching of its content. The membership was now integrated, welcoming not only African-Americans after an especially bitter civil rights struggle in Shreveport but also a global citizenry such as Vietnamese refugees. Women were ordained to serve as ministers and deacons, also providing leadership as the chair of key committees. Most important, members began to function as a priesthood of believers both to one another within the church and to outsiders beyond the church. With these changes firmly in place, it seemed that my little book had done the work which it advocated, thus I allowed it to go out of print once all available copies had been sold.

By the time I moved to Samford University in 1987, two contrasting developments made it clear that retiring the book was a mistake. On the one hand, my own denomination, the Southern Baptist Convention, erected high ideological walls that quickly divided a host of churches. Polarization replaced accommodation as the dominant dynamic in the public squares, intensifying the hostility displayed by religious groups aligned with competing political movements as they attacked one another.

On the other hand, at the same time that angry shouting triumphed over reasoned debate in the churches, surprising examples of reconciliation were taking place in the world. In 1990, after twenty-seven years in prison, Nelson Mandela was set free, signaling the end of apartheid where it was practiced most rigidly. The Iron Curtain dividing East and West collapsed without a shot being fired, moderating the Cold War that had defined a global balance of terror for an entire generation. Soon thereafter, the Soviet Union disintegrated, freeing whole countries from the grip of totalitarian Marxism. As the millennium drew to a close, it seemed to some that the secular quest for freedom might be more powerful than the Christian quest for unity.

In response to these developments, requests for the book steadily increased until used copies became scarce on the Internet. Pleadings of friends convinced me that a new edition was in order, particularly after I offered an intensive study of the material at the Mountain Brook Baptist Church in Birmingham, Alabama, where I have served as Theologian in Residence for twenty years. At first I envisioned an extensive revision and expansion, but these plans were necessarily abridged when, just as I began my work on this project, I was diagnosed with amyotrophic lateral sclerosis (ALS or "Lou Gehrig's Disease"), a degenerative malady that relentlessly diminishes one's strength. Faced with a fatal illness that has no known cause or cure, I decided to update the book where needed and to add a final chapter dealing with contemporary controversy, but to retain with little change the historical exposition that continues to reflect the findings of biblical scholarship. The basic thrust of the original edition has been left unchanged because of my conviction that it retains its relevance for the church of today.

In search of a controlling metaphor for what this book seeks to accomplish, I early settled on the imagery of Ephesians 2:14 which pictures the work of Christ as that of a wall-breaker. The immediate context in Ephesians 2:11-22 presents a breathtaking vision of the church as a New Temple resulting from his demolition activity. The daring claim is made that religion itself may need radical restructuring in order to reach its full potential.

The thrust of the text has required me to compare the New Testament understanding of its faith to that of the Jewish religion as it flourished in the first century of the Christian era, as well as to Roman Catholicism in subsequent centuries. Lest anyone misconstrue my resulting critique as even faintly reflecting the long history of anti-Semitism which has been a tragic chapter in Jewish-Christian relations, or of the Protestant-Catholic polemic prior to Vatican II, let me emphasize that I was forced to dwell on these points precisely because of a conviction that some of the same characteristics have reappeared today within my own Baptist community! In this study I hope that I am a persuasive advocate of Ephesian

Christianity, but I leave to my readers the decision of how they will apply this approach to their own religion.

I have chosen to treat a number of explosive themes, not because of any desire for controversy, but because their message is so central both to the New Testament and to the needs of our times. It has been no easier for the author than it will be for the reader to implement the daring vision set forth in our central scriptural text (Eph. 2:11-22). But even if we must do our work with the sound of detonations rumbling under the house of faith, in that hazardous venture lies the way to freedom, and thence to fulfillment, for all who are united and at peace in the body of Christ.

Acknowledgments

Because I have lived with the ideas in this book for more than a half-century, their development is beholden to more contributors than I can now remember or recount here. The present revision, however, was enriched by only a small circle of family and friends, due primarily to its composition while I was severely restricted by a degenerative disease.

Pride of place must go to our daughter, Susan Hull Walker. The rigorous training in which she excelled at Harvard Divinity School, plus a decade of pastoral leadership at a time when women ministers were still being judged more by their gender than by their ability, gave her a profound understanding both of what I was writing and of why I was writing it. My perseverance to complete this project owes much to the stimulus of her creative suggestions.

As has been the case with some of my earlier writings, Walter B. Shurden was most insistent and persistent that I begin work on this project and my dear wife, Wylodine, that I finish it! Between those motivational bookends, I was sustained by an extraordinary level of pastoral care from a host of friends, two of whom must be mentioned here. Close to home, a former seminary student of mine, James D. Moebes, anticipated and responded to my needs in practical and generous ways. I am delighted that the completion and dedication of this book coincided with his retirement after thirty years as senior minister in our congregation. Farther away, Duke K. McCall, now in his ninety-eighth year, made frequent use of the telephone to nourish and deepen a friendship that we have enjoyed throughout an adult lifetime.

I only hope that this book reflects in small measure the abundance of wisdom received from these cherished colleagues.

Once again, Joellen Henson brought her computer craftsmanship to this assignment. Since I can no longer talk or type, she was forced to begin by deciphering handwritten scratchings that I could barely read myself. In assuming several tasks that I could no longer perform, she was joined by our grandson, Andrew W. Hull, who volunteered to coordinate both the work of my caregivers and the maintenance of our home. Supplementing their work, which grows heavier with each passing day, James C. (Jace) Davidson checked the accuracy of quotations from Scripture and other primary sources.

I tell you a truth: without the help of those mentioned here, this book would not have been possible.

EPHESIANS 2:11-22

Remember, therefore, that in the past you were viewed as pagans in a physical sense, said to be "The Uncircumcised" by those who are styled as "The Circumcised" (a thing done to the flesh by hand). At that time you had no connection with Christ, being alienated from the commonwealth of Israel and strangers to its covenants of promise. Yours was a world without hope and without God.

Now, however, in union with Christ Jesus, all of you who were once faraway have become near through the blood of Christ. For he alone is our peace, he who has made both groups into one and has, by his earthly life, *broken down the dividing wall that formed a barrier of hostility between us*. It was he who transcended the Law understood as rules and regulations, so that he could fashion the two groups into one new humanity in union with himself, thereby achieving peace. His purpose, in other words, was to reconcile both groups to God in one body, and to do this through the cross, destroying thereby the hostility between them.

As I was saying, once he had come, he proclaimed peace to you who were far away and peace to you who were near. So, then, both groups alike now have access to the Father in one Spirit. This means, therefore, that you are no longer strangers and aliens but are fellow citizens with God's people and members of God's household, built upon the foundation of the apostles and prophets, Christ Jesus himself constituting the cornerstone.

In him the whole building that is being fit together grows into a holy sanctuary in the Lord. In him, every one of you are being built up together into a dwelling place of God in the Spirit.

Beyond the Barriers

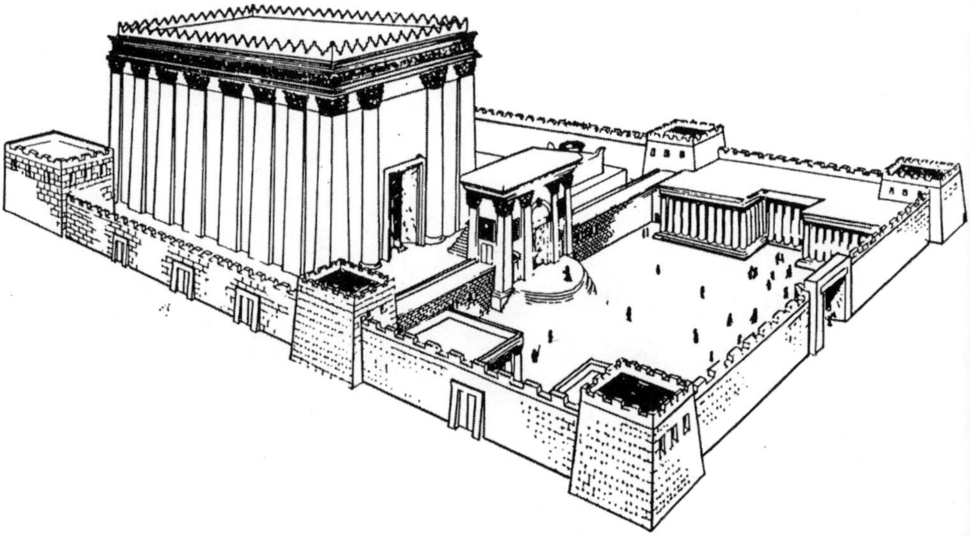

Herod's Temple from the East

1

The Wall Breaker

I

One of the most potent symbols of frustration in the twentieth century was a twenty-seven-mile-wide dagger driven deep into the heart of the brave but beleaguered city of Berlin. Thrown up between midnight on Saturday, August 12, and morning on Sunday, August 13, 1961, the Berlin Wall quickly became an outrage and effrontery to all who beheld it.[1] Marching insolently across proud plazas, invading ancient cemeteries, sinking its roots into buried sewers, this hideous barricade overnight condemned more than a million East Berliners to collective claustrophobia. In one stroke it literally amputated a great city through its midsection, severing those vital arteries through which the oppressed could flow in their quest for freedom. Mused a policeman assigned to this cockpit of the Cold War, "The Wall is not just sad. It is not just ridiculous. It is schizophrenic."[2]

Once erected, the ugly obstruction continued to grow under its own malevolent momentum, like a festering wound on the face of the city that would not heal. With ruthless

---

[1] For a comprehensive historical account see Frederick Taylor, *The Berlin Wall: A World Divided, 1961--1989* (New York: HarperCollins, 2006).

[2] "Wall of Shame," *Time*, August 31, 1962, 20.

efficiency its keepers added row after row of barbed wire, replaced nine-foot heaps of mortar with massive fifteen-foot concrete slabs (nicely whitewashed to provide a better backdrop for machine gunners), and installed a death strip replete with land mines, self-firing automatic weapons, vicious patrol dogs, antitank ditches, and steel spikes. Heroic attempts to conquer this fiendish obstacle course finally dwindled to a trickle as the 30,000 troops patrolling its no-man's-land gunned down at least 136 victims only a few feet from freedom.

And yet that infamous "Wall of Shame" in Berlin was but the most visible segment of a vastly larger cleavage dividing the world into hostile camps. Not only was it part of the 103-mile ring around West Berlin, sealing off that city as an island of freedom in a subcontinent of tyranny, but it also belonged to the 856-mile Iron Curtain stretching from the Baltic almost to the Balkans that partitioned not only Germany but also Europe into East and West. Here, again, the Wall continued to grow at a cost of $2,500,000 per mile, not in order to defend something else but to be defended itself. All of its deadly devices were turned in the wrong direction because they had been designed to destroy escapers, not invaders. Could any fortification be as obscene as this Marxist Maginot Line erected, not to restrain the enemy, but to imprison its own people!

Closer home, an invisible "Velvet Curtain" dropped protectively between affluent suburbs and inner city slums. Racial minorities still felt constrained by the "Jim Crow Curtain" of second-class citizenship. More recently, alarmed by the rising tide of illegal immigration, the United States committed $1.2 billion to build 650 miles of a fourteen-foot-high steel fence on the border with Mexico that will cover less than a third of the 1,952-mile boundary between the two nations. It is impossible to imagine all of the heartbreak that has gathered around those political, economic, and social barriers designed to stifle the human spirit. As Edith Lovejoy Pierce (1904–1983) put it:

> Walls are for weeping,
> Stones washed with tears,
> Heart's rain that does not dry
> Under high sun.
> Temple wall in Jerusalem,
> Kremlin wall, Berlin wall,
> Prison wall.
> Walls are for bleeding,
> Sadly dividing.
> Walls are for weeping,
> Stones washed with tears.[3]

The problem is compounded by a realization that cruel experiences of this world's walls may be internalized, that barriers to freedom and fulfillment may crisscross the terrain of mind and heart. Fear and insecurity, for example, often drive us to erect psychological bulkheads against the tides of change. Or prejudice causes us to encase our attitudes toward others in rigid stereotypes. One of the most impenetrable cordons of the emotions is quietly fashioned out of loneliness and isolation. The Greek poet, Constantine Cavafy (1863—

---

[3]Edith Lovejoy Pierce, "Wailing Wall," *The Christian Century*, July 31, 1974, 742.

1933), described how circumstances can conspire to isolate the self:

> Without consideration, without pity, without shame
> they have built big and high walls around me.
>
> And now I sit here despairing.
> I think of nothing else: this fate gnaws at my mind;
>
> for I had many things to do outside.
> Ah why didn't I observe them when they were building
> the walls?
>
> But I never heard the noise or the sound of the builders.
> Imperceptibly they shut me out of the world.[4]

This sensation of being hemmed in by walls, whether without or within, is called alienation. Because of real or imaginary barriers, we no longer feel truly in touch with our innermost selves, our neighbors, or even our God. Such a mood of disconnection is one of the dominant characteristics of contemporary culture.[5] Some suppose that our outward walls are built as a projection of our inward estrangement, while others reckon that the brutal fragmentation of society hastens the disintegration deep within. Doubtless there is a

---

[4]Constantine P. Cavafy, "Walls," *The Complete Poems of Cavafy* (New York: Harcourt, Brace & World, 1961) 17.

[5]For comprehensive anthologies on the pervasiveness of alienation in modern life see Gerald Sykes, ed., *Alienation: The Cultural Climate of Our Time*, 2 vols. (New York: George Braziller, 1964); Eric and Mary Josephson, *Man Alone: Alienation in Modern Society* (New York: Dell, 1962).

reciprocal relationship according to which each reinforces the other, which means that deliverance will be found only when we learn to dismantle both those external and those internal strictures that separate us from true freedom and fulfillment. That is but another way of saying that we cannot compartmentalize—that is, build a *wall* between!—the personal and the public dimensions of our existence.

II

In this wall-weary world full of people yearning to breach the battlements that stifle their spirits, suddenly a host of barriers began to crumble. Most amazing, the Berlin Wall itself was abolished without a shot being fired. Neither East Germany nor West Germany did anything to create an opening in the imposing barricade. Instead, both sides were so certain that the massive blockade was a permanent part of the geopolitical situation that neither had any contingency plans of what to do should it be dismantled. Just two months before demolition began, East German leader, Erich Honecker, boasted that the wall would stand for a hundred years. But when we ask what toppled the colossus, it seemed to be an accident, even a misunderstanding, as if the entire event were controlled by invisible forces that made the outcome inevitable.

The fall of the Berlin Wall provides a vivid illustration of how freedom has many unseen allies. In this case at least four major developments slowly but surely undermined the very foundations on which the Wall rested, so much so that, when its gates were first opened on November 9, 1989, surprising friend and foe alike, everyone immediately recognized that they could never be shut again. In a moment the mightiest bulwark in the world seemed to lose its power, becoming a playground for souvenir hunters. At first, when the wall was built, East Germans yielded to its restrictions with grim resignation fed by fear. But after a quarter century of multiple confinements, a younger generation began to sense new possibilities of liberation from the limitations of the past. Finally it was a collective will-to-freedom on the part of a broad cross section of East German citizenry that left the Berlin Wall defenseless. How did this happen?[6]

(1) *Political*. It began with solitary voices daring to call for change: Willy Brandt in West Berlin, Lech Walesa in Poland, and Václav Havel in Czechoslovakia. Soon individual courage found collective expression. By the spring of 1989 Poland held its first free elections since 1935, Hungary opened its border with neutral Austria, and Prague began to fill "freedom trains" bound for West Germany. Clearly a new momentum was building that the Berlin Wall had never before resisted.

(2) *Social*. For years the Warsaw Pact countries had acted in unison because all were satellites of the dominant Soviet Union. But suddenly new initiatives became possible to the consternation of East Germany because a fresh breeze was blowing out of Moscow. Using the watchwords *glasnost* ("openness" of speech) and *perestroika* ("restructuring" of the economy) the Soviet leader, Mikhail Gorbachev, was seeking to create a new mood of accountability throughout the Communist world. Rather than enforcing conformity by military might, each country was left to solve its own

---

[6]For a more comprehensive account of these developments and their immediate aftermath see Mary Elise Sarotte, *1989: The Struggle to Create Post-Cold War Europe* (Princeton NJ: Princeton University Press, 2009).

problems. For example, he refused to intervene despite increasingly desperate pleas from Soviet satellites. The Berlin Wall no longer had Soviet backing to enforce its demands.

(3) *Economic.* Forced to rely on its own resources for the first time, East Germany had to confront the long-denied fact that, for all practical purposes it was bankrupt. With massive indebtedness to the USSR for raw materials and to the West for technology, one of its few sources of hard currency was from the sale of political prisons as an "export item" to the West. No longer able to afford Polish black coal, the country began to burn its own supplies of brown coal called lignite, dramatically increasing pollution and giving buildings a dirty, decaying look. This slide into squalor, which accelerated during the 1980s, was dramatized for the populace by West Berlin television which daily showcased images of prosperity that the Berlin Wall could not censor. The command economy of Communism was on trial in the East, and the stark contrast between the two Berlins rendered a verdict that every East German could readily grasp.

(4) *Religious.* Clearly the climate was changing throughout the Soviet bloc in ways that would encourage expressions of hope for greater freedom on the part of ordinary citizens. Already Pope John Paul II had challenged Communism in the name of Christianity with significant results especially in his native Poland among the trade unions. In East Germany, one of the most powerful grassroots movements began as Monday evening meetings to pray for peace at St. Nicholas Church in Leipzig.[7] Beginning with a handful, the attendance

[7]The story is well told by Andrew Curry, "Before the Fall," *The Wilson Quarterly* 33/4 (Autumn, 2009): 16-25.

swelled to 600 in February 1988, but exploded in the fall of 1989. Thousands showed up to pack the church on September 4, twice that many the next Monday, the overflow scattered to meet in other churches. Soon the crowds had to take to the streets: 70,000 on October 9, 150,000 on October 16. The movement spread to churches in other cities, with more than 500,000 flooding East Berlin to rally on November 4. Efforts to suppress the movement were futile. As one observer remarked, the police were ready for everything except candles and prayers.

With the benefit of hindsight it is easy to assume that these four factors explain why the Berlin Wall fell.[8] What Henri Bergson called "the illusions of retrospective determinism" causes what actually happened to look as if it somehow had to happen.[9] To be sure, everyone knew that there was a yearning for freedom abroad in the land, but no one thought that it would threaten the Berlin Wall. Why? Because the Wall was a massive physical barricade to be penetrated by a superior physical force whereas all of this freedom ferment was but an intangible cry of the heart.

---

[8]This brief survey, concentrating on the Berlin Wall, does not attempt to identify factors influencing the wider global context, such as the Tiananmen Square protest in China and preparation to free Nelson Mandela from prison ending *apartheid* in South Africa. Many historians concluded that the events of 1989–1991 were so momentous as to mark the end of the twentieth century. Francis Fukuyama dared to suggest that this epoch signaled not just the end of the Cold War but "the end of history" in the sense of the universalization of Western liberal democracy representing the final form of human government. See his *The End of History and the Last Mass* (New York: Free Press, 1992).

[9]Timothy Garton Ash, "1989!," *New York Review of Books* (November 5, 2009): 4.

Slogans do not intimidate armed guards, candles do not shatter concrete, prayers do not stop bullets. That kind of contest was too absurd to be considered. By a huge failure of the imagination, neither side could see the power of the aroused human spirit simply to ignore the Wall as obsolete while overwhelming its keepers. Timothy Garton Ash has commented incisively:

> It is perhaps a characteristic of superpowers that they think they make history. Big events must surely be made by big powers. Yet in the nine months that gave birth to a new world, from February to November 1989, the United States and the Soviet Union were largely passive midwives. They made history by what they did not do. And both giants stood back partly because they underestimated the significance of things being done by little people in little countries."[10]

III

Despite the breakthrough in Berlin, ours is still a wall-weary world searching for those liberating forces that can overcome coercive restrictions confining the human spirit. In this quest for a demolition dynamic, Christianity is in danger of coming out second best. Consider those dominant images by which its faith is often conveyed to the world. All too often Christ is depicted in passive categories. At Christmas, he is a "babe lying in a manger" (Lk. 2:16). On Good Friday, he is a "lamb that is led to the slaughter" (Isa. 53:7). At Easter, he is an exalted Savior "seated at the right hand of God" (Col. 3:1). For

---

[10]Ash, "1989!," 8.

believers with biblical perspective these motifs have rich meaning in holy history, but for outsiders it is difficult to grasp how a sleeping babe, a suffering lamb, or a sitting Lord can do much about those obstructions that stifle our longing to be free.

To a world in search of wall-breakers, the apostle Paul provides a splendid corrective to the prevailing passivity in which many sincere Christians describe salvation. Seeking to capture the impact of Jesus' entire ministry in a single explosive phrase, Paul wrote in Ephesians 2:14, "He has *broken down* the dividing *wall* of hostility." How fitting that the savior bore the name "Jesus" (Aramaic, *Jeshua*), since this was a later form of the ancient Hebrew name, Joshua. Here was a new and greater than Joshua before whom walls mightier than Jericho came tumbling down (cf. Josh. 6:1-21). Behold the Great Abolitionist, cried the Apostle, God's demolition squad of one whose words were like crowbars that pried open unyielding gates and whose deeds were like bulldozers that leveled impregnable barriers. Far from being an unmoved deity such as the Greeks might imagine, God sent Jesus to abolish those very restrictions that thwart us to this day.

The metaphor of wall-breaker does not mean, however, that Jesus was some sort of spiritual storm trooper who rode roughshod over every obstacle to his cause. Paul clearly prefaced his claim with the announcement, "He is our *peace*, who has made us both *one*" (Eph. 2:14). That is, his work of dismantling walls was done, not as warrior, but as reconciler. Here was no iconoclast who loved to hear the sound of the wrecker's ball and see once beautiful masonry reduced to rubble. Rather, here was a mediator determined to provide "access" for the alienated by removing barriers which they had hitherto been unable to penetrate (Eph. 2:18). To this theme of the *con*structive rather than the *de*structive character of Jesus' work we shall return in chapter 6.

Shortly before the Ephesian description of Christ as a new Joshua was written, an Egyptian prophet appeared in Judea who sought to stir the masses into revolt against Rome. According to the contemporary Jewish historian, Josephus (*Jewish War* 2.261-63), this impostor urged those whom he could dupe to gather on the Mount of Olives where he wished to demonstrate "that at his command Jerusalem's walls would fall down, through which he promised to provide them an entrance into the city" (Josephus, *Jewish Antiquities* 20.170). This abortive effort at insurrection was quickly smashed by the Roman procurator, Felix, forcing the charlatan and his followers to flee for their lives. A short time later, Paul was mistaken for this messianic pretender (Acts 21:38), which is highly ironic because the Apostle knew better than anyone that it was not the Egyptian but Jesus who could level walls with a word, and that his purpose in so doing was not to wage war but to bring peace!

In order to understand the implications of this claim we must be clearer about the kind of wall to which the Apostle was referring. Although a number of allusions are possible, for details of which one may consult the commentaries,[11] the context establishes that the most likely reference is to the walls of the Jerusalem Temple. Ephesians 2:11-22 is a tightly knit passage of which our key verse is an integral part. The

---

[11]A thorough discussion by Markus Barth is in his monograph *The Broken Wall* (Philadelphia: Judson Press, 1959) 39-43, 154-60; and in his Anchor Bible commentary, *Ephesians*, 2 vols., AB 34, 34A (Garden City NY: Doubleday, 1974) 1:283-87.

basic structure of the paragraph is determined by a kind of personalized BC/AD comparison, the nature of life *before* Christ ("remember *when*" of v. 11) being contrasted with the nature of life *after* Christ ("but *now*" of v. 13). The central point of this contrast is that alienation, which was nowhere stronger than in the separation between Jew and Gentile, has been replaced by reconciliation through the uniting of these two groups in the Body of Christ. In order to depict this transformed relationship in spatial terms, the Apostle first pointed to the Jerusalem Temple with its "dividing wall of hostility" (v. 14), over against which he then painted a word picture of the church as a New Temple where there are no aliens or strangers but where every person is "builded together" (v. 22) into an indivisible whole.

If, however, our text intends to assert that it was the balustrade in the Jerusalem Temple that had been breached, then we are faced with an acute problem. For Paul was unequivocal in his claim that the festering impediment had already been torn down. He did not express the wish that Christ *could,* or the hope that he *would,* but rather the confidence that he *had* demolished those barriers which lay at the heart of his ancestral religion. Our difficulty stems from the fact that no Temple walls actually fell during the lifetime of Jesus. Indeed, they were still standing some thirty years later when Paul wrote these words. Certainly in no literal sense, or even in any obvious spiritual sense, had the Temple dividers been superseded as a result of the ministry of his Lord. It was business-as-usual on Mount Zion, just as it had been conducted for centuries, on the day when the Apostle made this audacious claim.

What, then, could Paul have meant by flying in the face of reality with an announcement that any pilgrim to

Jerusalem could readily verify as incorrect? Actually, the apparent absurdity of his declaration may be greater than we at first realize. For AD 61-63 is as good a period as any in which to date Ephesians,[12] and that is the very time when the Herodian Temple in Jerusalem was finally completed after a building program lasting more than eighty years![13] All over the Roman Empire the word must have gone out that, at last, the worship center was finished, filling the Jewish people with pride over their magnificent edifice. But in the imperial city a single Jew, stripped of all credentials but his prisoner's chains, dared to assert that the exciting report was false. The whole cultic system was indeed "finished," but not in the way that its devotees imagined. Those monolithic walls, which seemed stronger when Paul wrote than at any other time in history, already had a fatal flaw, appearances notwithstanding.

This means that our pivotal text is no engineer's report on architectural modifications made to the Jerusalem Temple by Jesus of Nazareth in the days of his flesh. Rather, it is a confession of faith by one of his followers based on how he

---

[12]Markus Barth, who has written the most exhaustive recent study of Ephesians, is representative of many scholars in concluding that, if Paul is the author, then "choices for the origins of Ephesians come down to Rome and the years 61-63, or to Caesarea two or three years earlier," of which "Rome, about 62, is the best guess for the origin" (*Ephesians* 1:51). Several scholars have concluded that Ephesians was written a generation later by a Pauline disciple but, if so, he would have been careful to reflect what the Apostle would have said had he lived long enough to write the epistle himself.

[13]The Herodian Temple was begun in 20/19 BC, the eighteenth year after Herod the Great began to reign as king of Judea in 37 BC (Josephus, *Jewish Antiquities* 15:380). It was completed under the procurator Albinus, who governed AD 62-64 (Josephus, *Jewish Antiquities* 20:219).

had actually seen Christ transform human relations, thereby creating an entirely new approach to the worship of God. The fact that the walls of the Temple did eventually collapse a few years later, leveled by the Romans in AD 70 never to be rebuilt again, had no real bearing on the ultimate truth of Paul's contention. J. Armitage Robinson has expressed well what the Apostle was claiming: "That barrier . . . was still standing in the Temple courts at the moment when St. Paul boldly proclaimed that Christ had broken it down. It still stood: but it was already antiquated, obsolete, out-of-date, so far as its spiritual meaning went. The sign still stood: but the thing signified was broken down."[14]

IV

We have now clarified that the crux of Christ's work was not to dismantle walls literally but to obliterate the hostilities which they fostered. This insight provides a bridge over which to journey in search of the relevance of our text for today. In the words of Robinson just quoted, if we can determine "the thing signified" which was broken down by the impact of Christ in the first century, then we shall be in a position to identify those walls, whether literal or symbolic, that signify the same obsolete realities needing to be swept aside by the power of his Spirit today. To do that, we need to take a closer look at the Jerusalem Temple, particularly its system of walls, in order to inquire regarding their intended

---

[14] J. Armitage Robinson, *St. Paul's Epistle to the Ephesians* (London: Macmillan, 1907), 60.

function. Join me, then, for a brief tour of the Temple areas as they existed in the time of Jesus and Paul."[15]

The Temple in Jerusalem was a parable in stone of the Jewish approach to God. The exclusivisms built into its very structure provided a physical expression in microcosm of the walled-in attitudes of those who gathered there to worship. The layout of the Temple, which was designed to reflect its theology, may be described as that of a Christian church turned inside out. Whereas Christians worship entirely within the church building, using the outside area only for landscaping and parking, the one place where Jewish worshipers never ventured was inside the Temple itself. Instead they worshiped on the outside in a series of courtyards carefully circumscribed by a cluster of surrounding walls. The Sanctuary proper was a very small building whose inside floor space (approximately 100 feet in length and one-third of that in width) made it about the size of a one-room country church. No more space was needed, even though this was the only Jewish Temple in all the world, because none but a handful of priests entered its outer chamber, the Holy Place, to perform a few assigned duties. The innermost chamber, called the Holy of Holies, almost

---

[15] Topographical surveys of the Herodian Temple abound in most Bible dictionaries and encyclopedias, of which one of the best is by W. F. Stinespring, *The Interpreter's Dictionary of the Bible,* 4 vols. (New York: Abingdon Press, 1962) 4:550-60. The standard monograph in English on Temple practices is the now-outdated work of Alfred Edersheim, *The Temple* (London: James Clarke, 1959 reprint). The most detailed architectural study is F. J. Hollis, *The Archaeology of Herod's Temple, with a Commentary on the Tractate "Middoth"* (London: J. M. Dent, 1934). For a recent study see Ehud Netzer, *The Architecture of Herod, the Great Builder* (Grand Rapids MI: Baker Academic, 2006) 137-78.

always stood empty, symbolizing that it was reserved as the dwelling place of God.

In front and to the sides of the Sanctuary proper lay four main courtyards, each of them elevated in relation to the others based on their proximity to the Sanctuary. Because of the increasing selectivity of those who could be admitted, the courtyards tended to become smaller as they approached the Sanctuary, yet all of them together were much larger than the building itself since the people actually gathered in these courtyards to participate in worship. Those coming up the Kidron Valley from Bethany through the Golden Gate and moving due west would find themselves successively in (1) the Court of the Gentiles, (2) the Court of Women, (3) the Court of Israel, and (4) the Court of Priests before reaching the steps that led into the Sanctuary. Separating these four courtyards were three walls of which we shall speak as the chapters of this study unfold. The first-century Jewish historian, Josephus, who was himself a priest, describes the overall arrangement and hints at its significance in the following summary:

> All who ever saw our temple are aware of the general design of the building, and the inviolable barriers which preserved its sanctity. It had four surrounding courts, each with its special statutory restrictions. The outer court was open to all, foreigners included; women during their impurity were alone refused admission. To the second court all Jews were admitted and, when uncontaminated by any defilement, their wives; to the third male Jews, if clean and purified; to the fourth the priests robed in their priestly vestments. The Sanctuary was entered only by the high

> priests, clad in the raiment peculiar to themselves. (*Against Apion* 2.102b-104)

What this brief description implies is that these walls on which we shall focus were not merely decorative but were determinative of Israel's basic understanding of the nature of religion. They did not serve simply to organize available space in convenient fashion; instead, they literally put each person in his or her proper place in relation both to others and to God. In so doing, they confirmed and reinforced assumptions that were operative wherever the Jewish religion was practiced throughout the world.

Nor is it surprising to find Paul saying that hostility was provoked by these walls, for in providing preferment of access to some, they inevitably denied it to others. As we shall see, the uniquely new thing about Jesus was not only his rejection of the distinctions maintained by these walls, but also his mission to provide equality of access both to God and to neighbors for every person regardless of who they might be by ethnicity, gender, or vocation.

We are not to suppose that first-century Judaism was necessarily more susceptible to wall building than other religions either then or now. Indeed, the more clearly we come to see what these walls represented, the more amazed we shall be to discover how tenaciously they still endure two thousand years after Christ came to tear them down. But the gospel is always heard as the glad affirmation that walls of hostility need not exist, that they have already been fatally undermined even when the final stone seems securely in place. In what follows we shall look first at these barriers in their first-century functioning, testing whether Christ actually fashioned new relationships that shattered old animosities.

Then we shall search for contemporary equivalents of alienation in our own religious systems and ask what it would mean to let the *new* Joshua do his same breakthrough work again today.

Lillian Smith concluded her spiritual autobiography, *The Journey*, in the hope that the day had come to overcome those ugly fissures that rend the common fabric of life:

I believe future generations will think of our times as the age of wholeness: when the walls began to fall; when the fragments began to be related to each other; when man learned finally to esteem tenderness and reason and awareness and the word which set him apart forever from other living creatures; when he learned to realize his brokenness and his great talent for creating ties that bind him together again.[16]

For those of us who believe that Christ has already fulfilled this hope in the lives of those who truly serve him, and that he can do as much for others who accept his reconciling work, the only adequate response is framed in the prayer of Carl Sandburg:

> Lay me on an anvil, O God.
> Beat me and hammer me into a crowbar.
> Let me pry loose old walls.[17]

---

[16]Lillian Smith, *The Journey* (New York: W. W. Norton, 1954) 255-56.

[17]Carl Sandburg, *The Complete Poems of Carl Sandburg*, rev. and exp. ed. (New York: Harcourt Brace Jovanovich, Inc., 1970) 109-10.

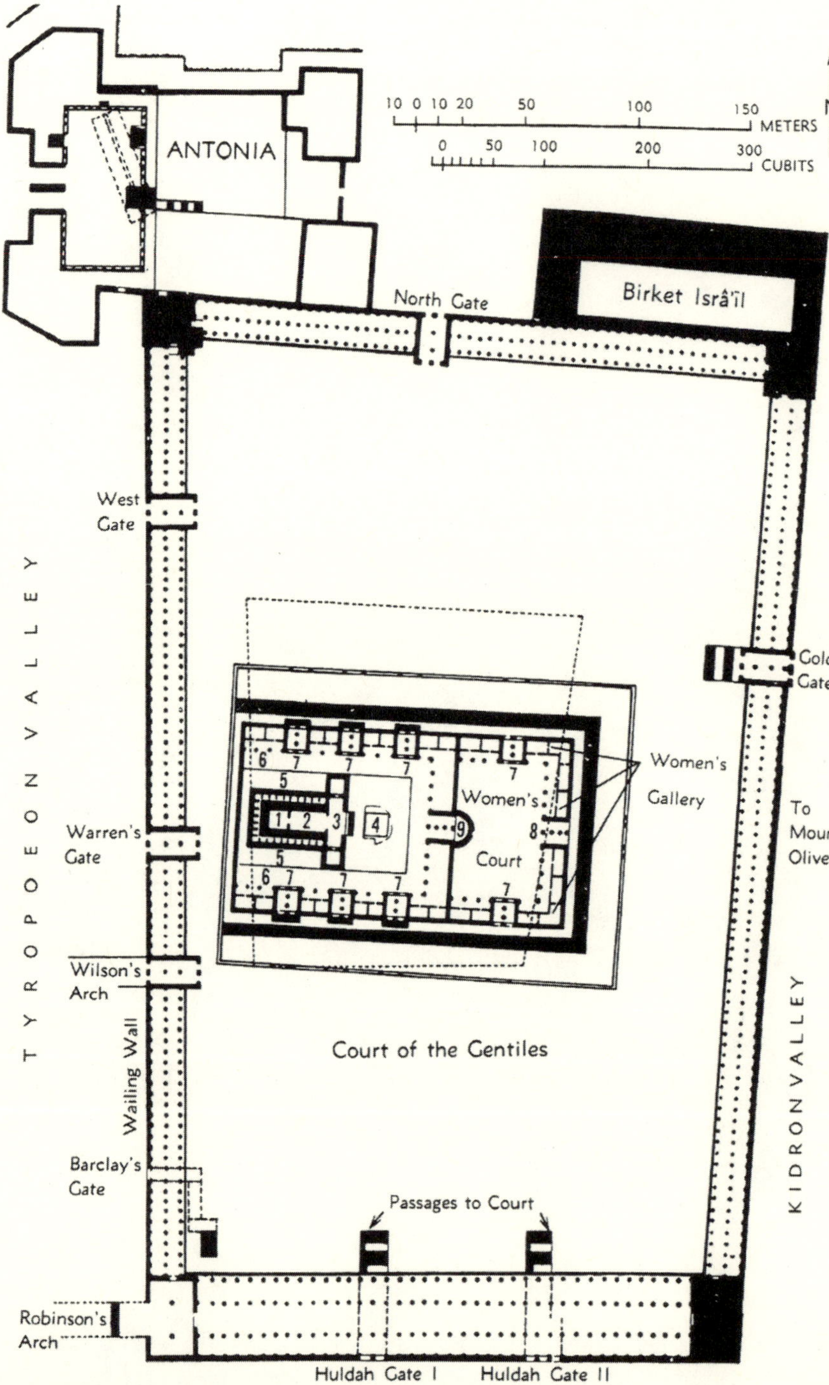

From Vincent and Steve, *Jerusalem de l'Ancien Testament* (Paris: J. Gabalda & Cie.)

34. Ground plan of Herod's temple and courts, based on Vincent-Steve: (1) holy of holies; (2) holy place; (3) porch; (4) altar of burnt offering; (5) court of priests; (6) court of Israel (men's court); (7) sanctuary gates; (8) Nicanor gate(?) or Gate Beautiful; (9) Nicanor gate

2

Beyond the Social Barrier

I

As our brief Temple tour in the preceding chapter indicated, worshipers in the New Testament period ascending to Mount Zion would find themselves first in the Court of Gentiles, the outermost, lowest, and largest of the four enclosures surrounding the front and sides of the Sanctuary. This platform was built up by Herod the Great to an irregular rectangle covering thirty-five acres, with outside measurements of 1,041 feet on the north; 1,556 feet on the east; 929 feet on the south; and 1,596 feet on the west. One reason for the great size of this trapezium stemmed from the fact that the term "Gentiles" meant "nations," which in Jewish usage referred to everybody else in the world! In other words, this precinct defined where all non-Jews could come to worship Israel's God.

A second reason why the Court of Gentiles dwarfed the Temple in size was somewhat ironic. The dimensions of the Sanctuary, going back to the time of Solomon, were modest indeed, but Herod gave assurances that they would be scrupulously followed as set forth in Scripture. At the same time he wanted the cultic complex to be his grandest building program rivaling the massive standards of Greek and Roman architecture. His ingenious solution was to make the Court of Gentiles, and therefore the entire Temple precinct, cover nearly thirty-six acres, larger than any comparable structure in the ancient world, to compensate for the small size of the Sanctuary itself.[1] The irony is that this huge space was not used primarily to reach multitudes of Gentiles but to provide Jews with such conveniences as living quarters for Levites, a synagogue for study, stalls for sacrificial animals, and tables for money changers.

Although extensive portions, on the north and south sides were accessible to foreigners, the Jews made clear that this entire terrace represented the most inferior section of their Sanctuary complex. For example, they referred to the total area including the Court of Gentiles as the "Temple Mount," but only to those smaller enclosures which were immediately adjacent to the Sanctuary building itself as the "Temple Court" (Mishnah, *Middoth* 2.1; 5.1). To be precise, the Court of the Gentiles "was merely the mount of the Sanctuary, not the Sanctuary itself. Therefore, Israelites who had been defiled by contact with a corpse, as well as non-Jews (in this respect of the same category as 'defiled' Jews), were permitted to enter it,"[2] Each component of the cultus was assigned varying degrees of sanctity, and, on a scale that calibrated ten grades of holiness, this area rated only the third grade, just above the land of Israel and the walled city of

---

[1]Carol Meyers, "Temple, Jerusalem," *The Anchor Bible Dictionary*, 6 vols., ed. David Noel Freedman et al. (New York: Doubleday, 1992) 6:365.

[2]Gustaf Dalman, *Sacred Sites and Ways* (London: S.P.C.K., 1935) 288. Actually, "Court of Gentiles" is a modern designation not used in the ancient sources, in part because the Jews did not wish to dignify this area with the title of "Court" since it was excluded from the true "Temple Court." For a detailed study see Yaron Z. Eliav, *God's Mountain: The Temple Mount in Time, Place, and Memory* (Baltimore: Johns Hopkins University Press, 2005) esp. 9-45.

Jerusalem, while all grades above that were reserved for other parts of the Temple (Mishnah, *Kelim* 1:6-9).[3]

Even more emphatic was the way in which non-Jews were prevented from venturing up to the Temple Court itself by a beautifully ornamented balustrade, or carved latticework screen, some four and one-half feet high.[4] The primary purpose of this partition was to segregate Gentiles from Jews in the worship of God. Nor was the provision of such a parapet unique to Judaism. "A pagan visitor had no reason to be offended in finding himself excluded from the holy ground. In all ancient religions there were sancta inaccessible to the profane crowd and separated by a rail of wood or stone."[5]

---

[3]For a detailed discussion of the ten degrees of holiness in this passage see Jacob Neusner, *A History of the Mishnaic Law of Purities* (Leiden: E. J. Brill, 1974) 1:37-44. Technically, one may count eleven rather than ten items in this ladder. I have resolved the problem by connecting the general reference to walled cities with the specific reference to the wall of Jerusalem and so counted the two of them together as the second level of sanctity.

[4]Josephus describes the wall as three cubits high (*Jewish War* 5:193). Since a cubit was approximately eighteen inches (the length of the forearm to the tip of the middle finger), this calculation would yield the four and one-half feet figure used here. However, the Mishnah pictures it as ten handbreadths high (*Middoth* 2:3). Since one handbreadth was considered a sixth of a cubit, or three inches, this would make the barrier only two and one-half feet tall. There is insufficient evidence to resolve the discrepancy. For a detailed discussion in support of the view that there may have been two walls at different times see F. J. Hollis, *The Archaeology of Herod's Temple, with a Commentary on the Tractate "Middoth"* (London: J. M. Dent, 1934) 153-57.

[5]Elias J. Bickerman, "The Warning Inscriptions of Herod's Temple," *The Jewish Quarterly Review*, n.s. 37 (1946-1947): 389; with numerous references both in note 12 and in the subsequent discussion on 389-90.

In the religion of the Temple, therefore, everything hinged on whether or not one were a Jew. But what did this involve? Then, as now, essential Jewishness was bafflingly difficult to define in simple terms. It included a *hereditary* factor, for all were considered descendants of Abraham, children of the twelve tribes of Israel. But it also included a *national* factor, citizenship in one commonwealth which claimed the right to rule the "Holy Land" of Palestine and maintain a capital in Jerusalem. Yet many Jews were dispersed in foreign countries where they were best able to show their solidarity by maintaining a common ethos: speaking the same language, obeying the same religious laws, and observing the same customs; hence there was a *cultural* factor as well. The combined factors of blood, soil, and lifestyle produced a sense of "people-hood" which understood Judaism as nothing less than a unified society. Hence, our first wall introduced into religion what we shall call, in the broadest sense, a *social* barrier.

II

Structures for maintaining Judaism as a distinct hereditary-national-cultural society flourished not only at the Temple but in every area of its religious life. During the first century, in the aftermath of the Maccabean crisis when the very survival of Judaism was threatened by assimilation into Hellenism, circumcision was emphasized more than ever before as the badge of belonging to the covenant of Israel. Not only was it required as the supreme rite of initiation for proselytes converting to Judaism (Josephus, *Jewish Antiquities* 20.38-48, 139, 145), but it was a profound sign of Jewish identity developed over centuries of religious usage. In the final chapter, we shall probe more deeply how this practice precipitated the most difficult controversy faced by the first Christians.

Hand in hand with an escalating emphasis on circumcision came the rising tempo of Jewish nationalism during the middle decades of the first century.[6] Already in the time of Jesus, the Zealot movement had gained popular support for its holy war to drive Rome from the kingdom that rightfully belonged to the sons of David.[7] Even the cautious Pharisees were openly questioning whether it was God's will to support the Roman state (Mk. 12:14). By the late fifties when the ministry of Paul reached its climax, Jerusalem was a powder keg of inflamed patriotism, so much so that any friendly association with Gentiles—even in Christian missionary service!—was now considered dangerous (Acts 20:3, 22-25; 21:10-13, 17-24). During the decade of AD 56-66, the revolutionary impulse in Jewish culture swept everything before it, which means that insurrection was in the air when our Ephesian passage was composed. No wonder it stressed the provision of "peace" between Jew and Gentile (2:14, 15, 17) and the nature of their relationship in the church as that of "fellow citizens" (2:19) in a new political order.

The most pervasive way that Jews showed their separation from other people was through the observance of Torah, those written commandments and oral traditions that

---

[6]The interrelation of circumcision and nationalism and their implications for the church have been movingly described by Dom Gregory Dix, *Jew and Greek* (London: Dacre Press, 1953) esp. 29-67.

[7]For an important study of this ferment see Martin Hengel, *The Zealots: Investigations into the Jewish Freedom Movement in the Period from Herod Until 70 A.D.* (Edinburgh: T. & T. Clark, 1989).

defined the way of God for Israel. Beginning with a nucleus in the Old Testament, specific prescriptions steadily grew by a process of interpretation and application into vast compilations called Mishnah, Gemara, and Talmud. Interestingly enough, the rabbinic responsibility of "making a fence around the Law" (Mishnah, *Aboth* 1.1), that is, of protecting it from contamination by surrounding it with correct teachings, led to the notion that the law itself was a protective wall guarding Israel from pagan corruption. The letter of Aristeas, for example, speaks of how "our lawgiver . . . fenced us about with impregnable palisades and with walls of iron, to the end that we should mingle in no way with any of the other nations" (139).[8] As Galatians and Romans make so clear, Paul had to struggle constantly against the tendency of the Law to do what the wall in the Court of Gentiles did at the Temple, namely to distance Jews from other peoples in their standing before God. This is why he closely tied the "breaking down of the dividing wall of hostility" by Christ (Eph. 2:14) to the "abolishing of the Law understood as a code of rules and regulations" (2:15) designed to foster Jewish particularism.

The paramount problem for Paul, however, was not the wall itself but the "hostility" that it engendered. Even as a Christian, he clung to the conviction that Israel had a unique place in the purposes of God (Romans 9-11). His dilemma was not that Jews were different, but that this difference had

---

[8]Moses Madras, ed. and trans., *Aristeas to Philocrates,* "Jewish Apocryphal Literature" (New York: Harper, 1951) 157. In the same paragraph, the writing continues, "so that we should be polluted by none nor be infected with perversions by associating with worthless persons, he has hedged us about on all sides with prescribed purifications" (142).

become divisive. Animosities first began to gather at the Temple 500 years earlier when it was being rebuilt after the Exile. So severe did tensions become under Ezra and Nehemiah that the Samaritans broke away and eventually established a rival temple on Mount Gerazim, which the Jews destroyed 200 years later (129 BC) under John Hyrcanus (Josephus, *Jewish Antiquities* 13.256). The desecration of the Jerusalem Sanctuary by Antiochus Epiphanes, and its subsequent restoration by the Maccabees, only intensified a feeling among Jews that Gentiles must never again violate its sacred space.

Suffice it to say, by the time of Jesus and Paul, more enmity had converged at our innocently beautiful balustrade than at any other religious spot on earth. Proof of the depth of these antagonisms was provided by the wall itself, for "at regular intervals stood slabs giving warning, some in Greek, others in Latin characters, of the law of purification, to wit that no foreigner was permitted to enter the holy place, for so the second enclosure of the Temple was called" (Josephus, *Jewish War* 5.194). Archaeologists have been fortunate to recover examples of these signs and thereby to confirm the ancient testimony that "death without appeal" was the penalty permitted by Rome for any foreigners—even Romans!—who passed the barrier (Josephus, *Jewish War* 6.126; *Jewish Antiquities* 15.417; Philo, *Embassy to Gaius* 212).

The most famous of these archeological finds is the warning inscription discovered by M. Clermont-Ganneau in May 1871.[9] Carved on a large limestone block (34 inches wide,

---

[9]Most of the reports by M. Clermont-Ganneau himself were in French, except for "Discovery of a Tablet from Herod's Temple," *Palestine Exploration Fund Quarterly Statement*, n.s. 22 (1871): 132-33. For pictures, text,

23 inches high, 15 inches thick) in letters more than one and one-half inches tall is this threat:

> No foreigner [Greek *allo-genes*, literally "one of any other kind, whether race, nation, or class"] may enter within the fence and enclosure surrounding the Sanctuary area. Whoever is caught so doing will have only himself to blame for the death which inevitably follows.

Note the ambiguity lurking in this syntax. The words do not say explicitly that the Jews would execute every trespasser apprehended, for the authority to do so without formal trial may have been ambiguous under Roman rule. Instead, the language implies that any Gentile who ventured further thereby took his life in his own hands! No one could miss the import of the message: "Stay out—or else!"

Lest we suppose this to be a rhetorical threat, deliberate exaggeration for the sake of emphasis, it is well to remember that Paul himself verified its sinister intention during his final trip to Jerusalem. Acts 21 records how, on the urging of local

---

translation, and interpretation of the inscription see J. Armitage Robinson, *St. Paul's Epistle to the Ephesians* (London: Macmillan, 1907) 160; Adolf Deissmann, *Light From the Ancient East* (New York: Harper, n.d.) 79-81 and fig. 9; Gustaf Dalman, *Sacred Sites and Ways* (London: S.P.C.K., 1935) 290; Jack Finegran, *Light From the Ancient Past* (Princeton NJ: Princeton University Press, 1951) 246 and fig. 111; C. K. Barrett, *The New Testament Background: Selected Documents* (London: S.P.C.K., 1956) 50; and Kurt Galling, "Middle Wall of Partition," *The Interpreter's Dictionary of the Bible*, 4 vols. (New York: Abingdon, 1962) 3:661 and fig. 22. More thorough than these representative introductions is the discussion by Bickerman, "The Warning Inscriptions of Herod's Temple," 387-405; with additions and corrections by Solomon Zeitlin, "The Warning Inscription of the Temple," *Jewish Quarterly Review*, n.s. 38 (1947--1948): 111-16.

church leaders, he went to extreme lengths to conciliate an explosive situation by demonstrating his support of the ancient Temple system (21:23-26). The plan backfired, however, when Jews who had already plotted against him in Asia (Acts 20:3) managed to incite a riot by stirring up the populace against Paul with the erroneous charge that he had "brought Greeks into the temple" and so "defiled this holy place" (Acts 21:28). Such an inflammatory accusation was based on the supposition that he had brought one of his Gentile companions, Trophimus the Ephesian, beyond the barricade. Without waiting to determine the truth of this charge, the masses became a mob that seized Paul, dragged him out of the Temple, shut the gates, and began beating him to death. Indeed, he would have been lynched in the shadow of the Sanctuary had not Roman soldiers intervened to save his life (Acts 21:27-32).

Let us be clear as to what happened here. Paul himself was a Jew with every right to enter beyond the Court of Gentiles; yet it was he, not Trophimus, who almost lost his life. Furthermore, this vigilante action by the Temple defenders was based, not on any evidence of an infraction by Paul, but on the merest suspicion that he might have been aiding and abetting non-Jews to profane the holy place. When Paul later wrote (to Trophimus, among others?) that this was a wall of *hostility*, he could point to his own experience for proof that he knew exactly what he was talking about!

III

Yet our text reflects the conviction of the Apostle, despite his traumatic encounter with the wall just a few years earlier, that Christ had long since shattered its effectiveness as a racially restrictive barrier. Obviously, the basis of his confidence lay not in any mellowing of attitude on the part of Judaism which, if anything, was becoming more belligerent as the showdown with Rome approached, but in the impact of the historical ministry of Jesus upon the repressive structures in which he had worked. Therefore, let us test the truth of Paul's contention by examining the way in which his Lord's life was hurled against the massive bulwark of separatism symbolized by the first Temple barrier.

Negatively, Jesus began with a strategy of silence. Joachim Jeremias has noted how he eliminated the Old Testament emphasis on revenge against the Gentiles from his proclamation of the messianic age.[10] In none of his teachings about Samaritans was there any hint of that implacable hatred which made Jewish pronouncements so contemptuous. Most significant, we find not a trace in all his recorded words of any advocacy of circumcision. In light of the temper of his time as sketched above, such an omission was about as incredible as if today a Baptist never mentioned immersion, a Catholic never spoke of the Mass, or a Pentecostal never referred to the Holy Spirit! In formal logic the argument from silence has limited weight, but in actual practice to say absolutely nothing in support of the burning watchword of the day can be deafening testimony indeed.

Positively, in place of circumcision Jesus championed faith as the bedrock of every person's access to God. But in that simple substitution he shifted religion away from its hereditary foundation. For faith, by its very nature, has

---

[10]Joachim Jeremias, *Jesus' Promise to the Nations,* Studies in Biblical Theology 24 (London: SCM Press, 1958) 41-46.

nothing to do with physical ancestry. If circumcision magnified the spiritual implications of a first or natural birth, then faith pointed to the necessity of a second or supernatural birth (Jn. 3:1-7). Here was an approach to God that ignored ancestry and nationality, both bulwarks of Jewish identity. That is why Jesus could commend a Roman centurion for reflecting such faith as he had not found anywhere in Israel (Matt. 8:10). Measured by circumcision, that army officer was an outsider, consigned to worship at the outer edges of the Jewish Temple. But measured by the criterion of faith, he was numbered among those Gentiles from every quarter who would sit down with the Jewish patriarchs to eat the messianic banquet in the kingdom of heaven (Matt. 8:11).

By championing faith as the sole channel of access to God, Jesus thereby put every person on equal footing and so universalized the potential membership of the religious community. But a necessary corollary to this axiom received equal emphasis from Jesus, namely, the boundless love of God. After all, unless God gives equally to Jew and Gentile alike, they cannot receive equally even if both make the same response of faith. No theme was clearer or dearer in the teaching of Jesus than the extravagant mercy of the Father to those inside or outside the religious pale of Judaism. When asked to explain why he welcomed sinners such as the despised tax collectors who did the dirty work for Rome (Mk. 2:13-17), Jesus replied quite simply, "Because God loves like that!—like a shepherd seeking his lost sheep, a woman searching for her lost coin, a father restoring his lost son" (cf. Lk. 15:1-32).

D. T. Niles has well summarized the ways in which Jesus showed equal concern for the good of all:

> We see how he broke down every single barrier that existed in his day between man and man, and interest and interest. He enlisted Simon the Zealot as a disciple, setting aside political distinction (Lk. 6:15). He dined with Zacchaeus, setting aside class distinction (Lk. 19:5). He conversed with the woman of Samaria, setting aside sex distinction (Jn. 4:27). He responded to the appeal of the Syrophoenician woman, setting aside race distinction (Mk. 7:26). He extolled the faith of the Centurion, setting aside national distinction (Matt. 8:10). He befriended sinners, setting aside popular distinction (Mt. 11:19). He allowed the woman who was a sinner to touch him, setting aside reputational distinction (Lk. 7:39). He praised the poor widow who gave her mite, setting aside economic distinction (Mk. 12:43). He washed his disciples' feet, setting aside the master-servant distinction (Jn. 13:14). He rebuked his disciples for their intolerance toward that follower who was not of the twelve, setting aside denominational distinction (Mk. 9:39). He enjoyed the company of children, setting aside age distinction (Matt. 21:15). His was a barrierless love.[11]

Not only was Jesus indifferent to the claims of circumcision that buttressed the hereditary basis of the Jewish religion, but he was equally unmoved by appeals from the Zealots to restore the national basis of their life by forcibly wresting it from the Romans. Jesus grew up in Galilee, the hotbed of this revolutionary movement, at the very time

---

[11]Daniel T. Niles, *That They May Have Life* (New York: Harper, 1951) 44-45 [with a correction of the final Scripture reference from Mark to Matthew].

when it was beginning to inflame the passions of the masses. After watching him feed more than five thousand, the populace was ready to "take him by *force* to *make* him *king*" (Jn. 6:15), but Jesus firmly sidestepped this frenzied neo-Maccabean draft. Nevertheless, this popular plea did not abate to the very end, as may be seen from the so-called triumphal entry which became a staged demonstration using Maccabean symbols that urged him to function as a warrior son of David in rescuing Jerusalem and its Temple from the hated domination of Rome (Mk. 11:1-10). Doubtless the greatest pressure of all came from within the disciple circle where "one of the Twelve—Simon the Zealot—*certainly* belonged to the Zealots; others *probably* did, like Judas Iscariot, Peter and *possibly* the sons of Zebedee."[12] Plausible as any is the theory that Judas betrayed Jesus in a misguided attempt to force him to assert his powers along lines advocated by the Zealots.

In spite of the most earnest entreaties calculated to appeal to his Jewish patriotism and pride, Jesus set himself steadfastly against every form of militant nationalism in the name of God. To him, "all who take the sword will perish by the sword" (Matt. 26:52). Most significantly, Jesus saw that even Jerusalem would not be spared in this suicidal collision course with Rome (Lk. 19:41-44; 21:20, 24; 23:27-30). If he could say of the Holy City, "See your house is left to you, desolate" (Matt. 23:38), this implied that even the Temple would be destroyed as well. Jesus chose an occasion when the disciples reflected the Zealot conviction of the inviolability of

---

[12]Oscar Cullmann, *The State in the New Testament* (New York: Charles Scribner's Sons, 1956) 17.

Mount Zion to make this explicit: "Do you see these great buildings? There will not be left here one stone upon another, that will not be thrown down" (Mk. 13:2). To utter such shocking words meant that Jesus foresaw not the revival but the end of all national life, even the semblance permitted by the Romans, for there could be no Jewish commonwealth as then understood without its unifying center in the Temple.

Equally sweeping was his assault on the third great bastion of Jewish exclusiveness, that intricate network of commandment and custom which rooted ultimately in the law of Moses. Jesus was a problem to his contemporaries because he seemed to work outside established sanctions for conduct: "By what *authority*," they kept asking, "are you doing these things, or who gave you this *authority* to do them?" (Mk. 11:28). Nor could there be any adequate answer because his authority came from within rather than from normative Jewish tradition in which the scribes found their authority (Matt. 7:29). The guardians of that precious heritage, the Pharisees, "were accused by their opponents of building a 'fence around the law,' and one of the opprobrious epithets applied to them was that of being 'builders of the wall'—i.e., builders of a wall around the Torah, fencing it in with the 'wall' of Pharisaic tradition."[13] For Jesus, the solution to this problem was not to break the Pharisaic monopoly by allowing alternative interpretations of the law, but rather to set aside all such accretions from any source and thereby stop

[13]Matthew Black, "Pharisees," *The Interpreter's Dictionary of the Bible*, 4 vols. (New York: Abingdon, 1962) 3:776. Some Jewish scholars have taken strong exception to this description of the Pharisees; e.g., Samuel Sandmel, *The First Christian Century in Judaism and Christianity* (New York: Oxford University Press, 1969) 101-102.

"making void the word of God through your tradition which you hand on" (Mk. 7:13). As a step in that direction he deliberately violated Jewish religious regulations in an effort to force a discovery of the will of God which undergirded them (Mk. 2:23--3:6).

Only a true Jew can grasp the revolutionary import of what Jesus achieved "he has abolished the law with its commandments and ordinances" (Ephesians 2:15). Joseph Klausner was one such modern Jew who saw the issue well. Let us listen to him at some length, without rejoinder, in an effort to feel the force of a development which, for Jesus' contemporaries, must have been devastating indeed:

> *Judaism is not only religion and it is not only ethics: it is the sum-total of all the needs of the nation, placed on a religious basis....*
>
> Judaism is a national life...Jesus came and thrust aside all the requirements of the national life;...in their stead he set up nothing but an ethico-religious system bound up with his conception of the Godhead.
>
> In the self-same moment he both annulled *Judaism* as the *life-force* of the Jewish nation, and also the nation itself as a nation. For a religion that possesses only a certain conception of God and a morality acceptable to *all* mankind, does not belong to any special nation, and consciously or unconsciously, breaks down the barriers of nationality.[14]

Near the climax of his ministry, the Synoptic Gospels record how Jesus went up to Jerusalem to test the readiness of the Temple to transcend heredity, nationality, and tradition, and so to function as a universal center of worship in the New

---

[14]Joseph Klausner, *Jesus of Nazareth* (London: George Allen & Unwin, 1925) 390, with further stimulating comment on 391-97.

Age which was soon to dawn. Entering the Court of Gentiles, he found not a worldwide pilgrimage of all peoples to Mount Zion, which even Jewish prophetic thought pictured in connection with the messianic era (Isa. 25:6-8),[15] but dealers in unblemished animals used for sacrifice, money changers who converted Roman coinage into local shekels used to pay the Temple tax, and patrons of these enterprises, some of whom were using the Temple as a thoroughfare between the western and eastern parts of the city (Mk. 11:15-16). His response was to repudiate the entire arrangement by which business-as-usual had usurped the centrality of worship, and routine ritual had become a substitute for worldwide compassion. By means of two prophetic passages Jesus explained his condemnation of the Temple for its colossal failure to be "a house of prayer *for all the peoples*" (Isa. 56:7); instead, it had become "a den of robbers" (Jer. 7:11) where Gentiles were being robbed of their ultimate right to meet God without any hindrance (Mk. 11:17).

This frontal attack on the Temple cost Jesus his life. Finally, the only charge his enemies could make stick was a distorted accusation, which did contain a grain of truth, to the effect that he was trying to destroy their Temple (Mk. 14:58). Considering the fact that business returned to normal only hours after Jesus had swept the outer court clean of its holy hucksters; plus the fact that the adoring multitudes quickly proved that they wanted no part of a Temple-destroyer (Mk. 15:29); plus the fact that Stephen, the first disciple to take up the message of Jesus against the Temple (Acts 6:13-14), was

---

[15]Jeremias, *Jesus' Promise to the Nations*, 55-77, with numerous citations of relevant Jewish literature.

promptly stoned to death for so doing (Acts 7:48, 58), we may ask in all candor: Did Christ destroy the wall, or *did the wall destroy him*?

The answer to that question was not long in coming. Jesus had died on the cross for a faith purged of its particularism. As the epistle to the Hebrews argues, outside the city wall, at a place called Calvary, things such as parentage and citizenship and reputation suddenly mattered not at all (13:12-14). Soon that faith arose in the lives of his followers. The book of Acts traces in swift strokes how they began to liberate Christianity from its Jewish womb: first to Samaritans (8:1-25), then to an Ethiopian eunuch (8:26-40), then to the God-fearer Cornelius (10:1 to 11:18), then to Greeks in Antioch (11:19-26), finally to Gentiles everywhere (15:1-35). By the time of Galatians, one of Paul's earliest letters written some twenty years after the ministry of Jesus, the apostle could look back on an accomplished fact and cry, "There is *no longer Jew nor Greek,...* for all of you are *one* in Christ Jesus" (Gal. 3:28).

To be sure, Judaism had made progress toward a universal religion by providing a place for other peoples within the Temple structure. The Jews would never say that foreigners did not deserve to know their God; rather, they only insisted that non-Jews worship the one true God from a distance—"in their place" on the outer periphery. The Christian difference was one of taking this Jewish beginning to its ultimate fulfillment by providing for all races, nations, and cultures without any barriers at all. It is simply a fact of history that in less than one generation a movement that began within a highly developed hereditary-nationalistic-particularistic religion emerged to embrace those of every ancestry, citizenship, and culture without distinction. All over the Greco-Roman world, Christian communities began to spring up as a new kind of Temple (cf. 1 Cor. 3:16; 2 Cor. 6:16; Eph. 2:21-22) where the walls were down so that "one new humanity" might emerge (Eph. 2:15b).

IV

Today, it would seem, the first-century situation is completely different. There is no longer a Jewish Temple in Jerusalem; in its place stands a Muslim shrine, the Mosque of Omar (Dome of the Rock), over which property the Jews do not even preside. Instead of the Herodian Sanctuary with its many walls, Jews today meet for worship in synagogues that often resemble Christian churches. Then can we say that time and circumstance have served to heal ancient animosities, so that our primary concern has become anachronistic? At a more practical level, does it matter any longer what Jewish attitudes and practices were two thousand years ago? Should contemporary Christians, unlike their New Testament counterparts, simply ignore Judaism in pursuing an approach to God, so that the kinds of issues raised here become irrelevant, and therefore obsolete?

Although it would be temptingly convenient to answer in the affirmative, the truth is that we cannot go about our business as if the problem of Temple barriers no longer existed. For the realities that they represented have now crossed over from the parent faith and entered into the mainstream of Christian thought and practice. Ironically, the restrictive practices that Judaism developed and the hostilities that they engendered when it was once a dominant religion in Palestine have become characteristic of Christianity where it is now a dominant religion. No two situations are ever the same, but striking parallels suggest that those ancient walls in Jerusalem may be sturdier than we at first supposed.

For example, consider the ways in which Christianity has fostered a religion with a strongly hereditary basis. Sunday morning is still the most exclusive hour of the week as typical congregations gather for worship only with "our kind" of people. Until quite recently, particularly in the American South, exclusion from fellowship by virtue of race was not only compulsory but engendered deep hostilities on both sides of the barrier. Caught up in that turmoil that attended the integration of public life, many church folk momentarily forgot that their guidelines come from the Bible, not the newspaper, and rushed in defiance to bar the doors of their sanctuaries lest a handful of "agitators" be admitted.

Now that the anger has abated and the demonstrations have ceased, perhaps we can begin to appreciate the irony of those bristling confrontations. In most Christian churches today there is scarcely a Jew to be found. In the worship services of my denomination, for example, almost everyone present has long been White-Anglo-Saxon-Protestant, which, being interpreted, means a room full of Gentiles! There we were, "The Uncircumcised," who by genealogy had no right to be inside the sanctuary in the first place, trying to tell another ethnic group, non-Jewish like ourselves, that they would have to stay out! The point is obvious; if we were determined to restore the Jerusalem Temple rationale, with its requirement of hereditary qualifications for admission, then, to be consistent, all of us Gentiles—whether white or black—would have to stand together on the outside and allow only Jews to move in closer beyond the outermost vestibule.

Occasionally one still hears, fortunately with diminishing frequency, the retort that all peoples are entitled to worship

God "in their place." Such language smacks of the old Temple, with its barriers firmly entrenched, not of the new Temple where distinctions between "Jew and Greek" have been transcended. The limitations of that reactionary stance should be apparent just by looking around at the congregation in a typical Christian sanctuary and realizing that this varied group of Gentiles would never have gotten where it is if Christ had not long ago demolished social distinctions, liberating his movement to spread throughout the world by offering equal opportunity to all who believe. Those with a lingering residue of racial apartheid in their religious outlook would do well to pause each time they enter freely into a Christian worship center and ask, "How did *I*, with *my* non-Jewish heritage, ever get admitted to this place?" The only honest answer, of course, is: "Because my Lord nullified the whole rationale for restricting equal access to God by virtue of ancestry."

It is the same situation when we turn from the relation between religion and heredity to that between religion and nationality. Still the Zealots are among us who would identify Christianity so closely with the American way of life that the political enemies of our country become the spiritual enemies of our faith. As recently as the anti-Communist crusades of the Cold War era, the assumption almost triumphed that everyone unfortunate enough to live under the banner of a hated foe (e.g. all Russians) must be lumped together as adversaries and placed on the far side of a wall where hostilities rage. During the high tide of the McCarthy inquisition in the 1950s, anyone foolish enough to reach across that nationalistic barrier in a spirit of Christian love was immediately denounced as a "Communist sympathizer" and added to a purge list that might well lead to the loss of reputation, employment, and peace of mind.

Today the intensity of contemporary zealotism fluctuates more in response to the political climate than in response to informed Christian conviction. What those who would absolutize political fervor in the name of God fail to recognize is that God himself is not hemmed in by national boundaries. His compassion does not travel on an American passport, nor does it enter only those lands to which we extend diplomatic recognition. Our theology must be determined, not by a decision made in Washington regarding our nation's enemies, but by a decision made on Calvary to die for all the world (Jn. 12:32). If citizens of any country have Christ in common with those of another country, then they are "both *one*" and have "peace" between them (Eph. 2:14) even if their respective nations are viewed as belligerents.

There are at least three obvious ways in which we may bear witness to a religion without national barriers. One is by living in loyal but creative tension with the claims of our own country. It is common to refer to the Church *of* England or to the First Baptist Church *of* Shreveport. This usage symbolizes a subtle but serious mistake. The New Testament characteristically speaks of the church *in* Corinth or of the church *in* Rome, for the church is to be *in* but not *of* the country or city where it lives. Another suggestion is to study, pray, and contribute as strong supporters of a truly worldwide missionary endeavor that does not "follow the flag" as the vanguard of American imperialism but seeks "to become all things to all people" (1 Cor. 9:22), as did Paul, including those unfortunate enough to have been born under a totalitarian Roman regime. Finally, we may seize every opportunity for international fellowship that demonstrates our transnational solidarity in Christ. In my denomination, for example, the Baptist World Alliance sponsors every five years a World Congress at which believers from all the nations represented affirm their solidarity in Christ with a love for one another that many harried diplomats of this world can only envy.

We have seen that in the first century there was not only a hereditary and national, but also a cultural component to the wall of Gentile exclusion, and the same is true today. At one extreme, the Roman Catholic Church has legal regulations in its canon law that, through the centuries, has grown to the proportions of the Jewish Talmud. The formal binding character of church legislation is not as strong in the Protestant tradition, although conflicting regulations kept Lutherans and Presbyterians debating how to observe the Lord's Supper for 400 years! The evangelical churches glory in their exclusive devotion to the Bible which frees them from all ecclesiastical tradition, but then they promptly forget that ideal in endless debates over biblical interpretation which often mean little more than: "What has been the traditional attitude and practice of the majority in this part of the country during the past fifty years?"

All that we are doing here is pointing to the persistence and power of religious tradition by whatever name and in whatever form. Christian history both within and between denominations is a sad story of bickering over theological catchwords that may have no centrality at all in Scripture. But beyond such official debates to which the laity pays little attention, the real strength of custom and convention is seen in the binding patterns of lifestyle that can consign a church to cultural captivity. Hardly noticed and never mentioned, an almost overpowering ethos can settle over a congregation that sends out such signals as: only upward achievers (no ghetto victims) welcome here; only white-collar eggheads (no blue-collar hardhats) welcome here; only stable families (no shattered divorcees) welcome here. On and on the list might go, limited only by the cultural options in our pluralistic society.

Of all the barriers designed to keep outsiders at arm's length, the cultural is the hardest to tear down both because it is so pervasive and because it gets so completely intertwined with our deepest values. One's ancestry and nationality are fairly obvious, commonly recognized realities whose influences may be readily identified and, to that extent, controlled. But one's lifestyle is an imperceptible blend of conviction and custom, morality and mores, with honest Christians debating where one stops and the other begins. For example, is the difference between "conservatives" and "moderates" a matter of intellectual training and temperament, and therefore a cultural phenomenon to be transcended, or is it an essential issue of faith which should run like an impregnable battlement dividing Christians into warring camps? Again, is the difference between total abstinence and the temperate use of alcoholic beverages a matter of environmental background, since the same Christian groups take opposite positions in America and in Europe, or is it an ethical absolute which should separate the children of light from the children of darkness? I have chosen these random examples, not to endorse a particular position, but to show how eager many Christians are to build monolithic "walls of hostility" at those junctures where our religio-cultural practices differ.

Both the difficulty of the issue and a direction toward its resolution may be discerned from Paul's letter to the Galatians, the most sustained and impassioned argument in

Scripture for a Christianity without cultural restrictions. To the Apostle, *anything* other than faith in Christ as a response to the grace of God was secondary and, therefore, ultimately superfluous (Gal. 2:15-21). When he came to specifics, Paul was prepared to jettison such things as circumcision (5:2-12) and the festival days prescribed by the religious calendar (4:8-11), even though both were enjoined repeatedly in Scripture. If we flinch before the call to freedom stated here with such radical comprehensiveness (5:1), it may be well to remember that we are the direct beneficiaries of his courage. After all, circumcision and Passover observance have long since lost their binding force in *our* churches. The real question, therefore, is whether we are prepared to apply that same courage to the liberation of our faith from contemporary practices that may have begun as bridges to God but have long since become barriers separating us from others.

One caution may help to clarify just where courage is relevant and to distinguish it from mere rashness. Nothing that has been said here about leveling ancestral, national, and cultural walls means that ethnicity and citizenship and tradition are wrong in themselves. There is not anything particularly Christian about rejecting one's seed or soil or society. Indeed, to ignore homeland and heritage is to become some kind of ahistorical person, which is the antithesis of Christian incarnational realism. The very fact that Jesus had a strong sense of belonging to a certain people, of living at a specific time and place, of working within an inherited system that had taken centuries to develop, means that God fully honors our "allotted the times of their existence and the boundaries of the places where they would live" (Acts 17:26). It is finally Gnostic, not Christian, to attempt to become so "universal" that we recognize none of the particularities of the created order.

Therefore, we may certainly rejoice in the achievements of our ethnic group; "red and yellow, black and white" are *all* beautiful. Let an unashamed patriotism for the best in our nation's ideals nourish a responsible citizenship. Let us strive to develop those structures that make for an open, yet stable society. But, let us never confuse any of these things with our religious standing in the sight of God or of others. The fatal mistake comes when we try to universalize the particular, absolutize the relative, and perpetuate the transient, thereby making divine (that is, "religious") that which is merely human, rather than setting the two in creative tension. The problem with Klausner's view of religion quoted above, or that of those like him, whether Jew or Christian, who would define religion as the life-force of a particular people rather than as a universal vision available to all mankind, is that this view so completely historicizes religion that it can no longer function dialectically as the presence of the eternal in the midst of time.

Those weary with the weight of history may wonder if any earthbound institution, even a temple/church which lives on the boundary between heaven and earth, can ever reflect, not its own surroundings, but the realities of the world to come. This is the decisive question on which Christianity stands or falls. To be sure, it requires a miracle for our worship to transcend the tired cleavages of time, but Christianity affirms that such a miracle has already been given in the finished work of Christ.

3

Beyond the Sexual Barrier

I

Resuming our tour of the Temple precincts, we leave behind the Court of the Gentiles with its segregation along social lines. Looming up in the west-central section of this large enclosure was a massive wall some sixty feet high within which lay the elevated "holy place" itself, a rectangular area 483 feet long on its north and south sides and 202.5 feet wide on its east and west sides. This summit was approached first by climbing fourteen steps, then crossing a level rampart fifteen feet wide that surrounded the quadrangle, then proceeding from this raised causeway up an additional flight of five steps through nine gates, four of which were on the north, four on the south, and one on the east.

This section of the Temple was subdivided into an inner court and an outer court. The inner, which we shall consider later, was the larger of the two. Measuring 280.5 feet by 202.5 feet, this is where the Temple service itself was conducted. The outer, with which we are concerned here, was 202.5 feet square. This is where Jewish men and women gathered for worship. It came to be called the Court of Women, not because it was assigned for the exclusive use of the daughters of Israel, but because "women were forbidden to enter... beyond the partition wall" into the sacred space where only Jewish men might venture (Josephus, *Jewish Antiquities* 15.419;

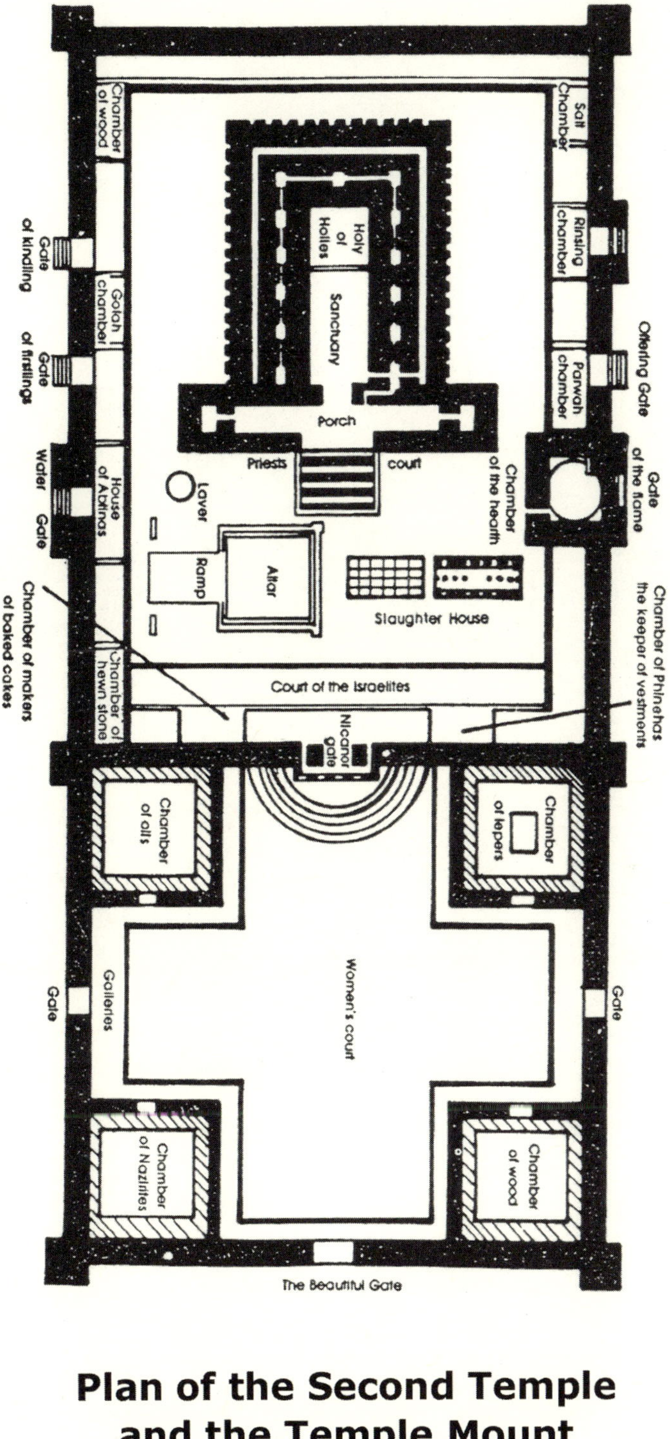

Plan of the Second Temple and the Temple Mount

Jewish War 5.199).[1] Here, then, we encounter a second obstruction rooted in the theology of the Temple architecture, which introduced a distinction between males and females into their "standing" before God and hence their "place" within the commonwealth of Israel. This partition based on gender symbolized what we may call the *sexual* barrier in religion.

Everything about the physical arrangements in the Court of Women was calculated to underscore the inherent inferiority of females in the worship of God. Of the nine gates opening from the terrace above the Court of Gentiles up to the holy place, only three led into the Court of Women (one each from the north, east, and south), the other six leading directly to the inner area where women were not welcome. All around the sides of the women's court, against the wall, were thirteen chests where charitable contributions were placed. These receptacles were narrow at the mouth and wide at the bottom, this horn-like shape suggesting why they were called "trumpets." We know from the Gospels that men and women alike streamed into this "treasury" to deposit their offerings, sometimes with no little fanfare on the part of those who could give more impressive sums than poor women (Mk. 12:41-44; cf. Mt. 6:2).[2]

Despite the small size of the Court of Women, at each of its four corners were enclosures without roofs measuring

---

[1]The physical characteristics of the Court of Women are described by Josephus, *Jewish War* 5.195-205 and *Jewish Antiquities* 15.417-18; and by the Mishnah, *Middoth* 2.5.

[2]Alfred Edersheim, *The Temple* (London: James Clarke, 1959) 48-49, who describes the specific objects to which the gifts were devoted as clearly marked on each trumpet.

sixty feet square. If dimensions given in the Mishnah are accurate (*Middoth* 2.5; cf. Ezek. 46:21-24), these four corner chambers occupied thirty-five percent of the available floor space![3] The one to the northwest was the Chamber of Lepers where males purified of skin diseases washed themselves before seeking admittance to the inner court (Mishnah, *Negaim* 14.8; cf. Mk. 1:44). The one to the northeast was the Chamber of Wood where priests unfit for other service because of bodily blemishes picked worms out of the wood destined for the altar. The one to the southeast was the Chamber of Nazirites where this group cooked their peace offerings and burned their hair clippings by throwing them in the fire under the pot (Num. 6:18). The one to the southwest was the Chamber of Oils where supplies of oil and wine were stored for use in the candlestick and with the offerings. The scene depicted by these arrangements was one of considerable noise and stench, with which the women who gathered for worship were not involved but which they could hardly avoid!

Partly because of crowded conditions, but even more for theological reasons, Jewish females were further segregated, even within their own court, by being placed in a gallery or elevated balcony, especially during the Feast of Tabernacles (Mishnah, *Sukkah* 5.2), "so that the women should behold from above and the men from below and that they should not mingle together" (Mishnah, *Middoth* 2.5). The Tosefta quotes

[3]Because the four corner chambers would take so much of the available courtyard space if they were located inside the enclosure, Hollis argues that they stood outside its walls. F. J. Hollis, *The Archaeology of Herod's Temple, with a Commentary on the Tractate "Middoth"* (London: J. M. Dent, 1934) 188-89.

Zechariah 12:12, "The house of David by itself, and their wives by themselves" in opposition to the mingling of the sexes in public gatherings.[4] (Incidentally, the segregation of the sexes for worship was carried over from the Temple to the synagogue services and in Orthodox Judaism continues to this day.)

In modern Jerusalem, nothing of the Temple remains except foundation stoves laid by Herod to build up the top of the Temple Mount so that it would accommodate a more expansive building program. Today the Western Wall, which best exposes these remnants, has become an iconic Jewish holy site and the adjacent space a central place of worship. Orthodox rabbis in charge of these services, in an effort to perpetuate the ancient past, have ruled that women may not sing aloud, carry a Torah scroll, wear a prayer shawl, or sit with men at worship. A group called Women of the Wall, organized in 1988 to protest these restrictions, lost their appeal before the Israeli Supreme Court, after which they were banished to conduct services in an archeological garden out of sight of worshipers in the sacred space. Any violation of prevailing practices is now considered criminal behavior subject to arrest.[5]

In our discussion of the Court of Gentiles, it was pointed out that the Jews used ten grades of holiness to make subtle distinctions regarding the degrees of sanctity assigned to various parts of the Temple. The first, or lowest, grade was the land of Israel; the second was the walled city of Jerusalem;

---

[4]J. D. Eisenstein, "Gallery," *The Jewish Encyclopedia* (New York: Funk & Wagnalls, 1910) 5:555, citing the Tosefta on *Sukkah* 4.1.

[5]Isabel Kershner, "Challenging Tradition at the Heart of Judicism," *New York Times*, December 22, 2009, A-8.

the third was the Temple Mount where Gentiles gathered; the fourth was the elevated terrace or rampart surrounding the Temple proper; while the fifth was the Court of Women which we have been describing here (Mishnah, *Kelim* 1.6-9). But this outer court was clearly less sacred than the inner court, from which women were excluded, where the Holy Place was considered to begin and within which the five highest grades of holiness were to be found.

Jewish tradition had implemented the command in Numbers 5:2 to keep the camp in the wilderness pure by dividing the Tabernacle into three grades of sacredness: the camp of Israel, that of the Levites, and that of God. Because the Tent had long since been superseded by the Temple, corresponding divisions were applied to the Holy City, as follows. From the outer walls of the city to those of the Court of Gentiles was the lowest "camp of Israel." From there to the walls of the inner court of the Sanctuary was the middle "camp of the Levites," while from there into the Holy Place itself was the "camp of God" or Shekinah's (lit. "dwelling" [of God]) camp. Obviously, the placement of the Court of Women in the second or Levites' camp reflected its valuation as a halfway house in the approach to God.

II

We are now ready to move beyond historical description, both architectural and theological, by asking *why* this sexual barrier was such a significant fixture of Temple worship. Our answer must be: because it symbolized the role of women in

Judaism as second-class religious citizens.[6] This situation stemmed from no distinctive spiritual conviction but was based on the subordination of the female to the male in every area of Jewish life.

From the earliest days of the Hebrew family, a woman was usually subject to a man throughout life: to her father if single, to her husband if married, or to her husband's brother if widowed. Her legal rights were severely restricted by male privilege: The husband could repudiate her but she could not divorce him (Deut. 24:1-4). She had no rights of inheritance even if there were no male heirs (Num. 27:1-11). Responsibility for a levirate marriage could be spurned by an obstinate man willing to endure public disgrace but the woman had no such choice (Deut. 25:5-10). Even her religious vows unto the Lord could be nullified by father or husband if he disapproved (Num. 30:3-15).

Although the social standing of women slowly improved with advancing civilization, her religious role continued to be diminished in the rabbinic Judaism of the New Testament period. On the positive side, polygamy gradually gave way to monogamy, largely out of economic necessity, although the rich and powerful could still maintain themselves in patriarchal style. For example, Josephus tried to explain the many marriages of Herod the Great by commenting that "it is an ancestral custom of ours to have several wives at the same time" (*Jewish Antiquities* 17.14). Despite these excesses, mar-

---

[6]The analysis which follows reproduces some material from the author's hermeneutical essay, "Woman in Her Place: Biblical Perspectives," *Review and Expositor* 72 (1975): 5-17. For a more comprehensive survey relevant to this entire chapter see Evelyn and Frank Stagg, *Woman in the World of Jesus* (Philadelphia: Westminster Press, 1978) esp. 13-100.

riage and procreation were exalted as the duty of every loyal Jew. Stricter movements opposed both premarital and extramarital intercourse, as well as all forms of deviant sexual behavior. Although divorce remained largely a male prerogative, permissiveness in repudiating a wife was severely curtailed by the school of Shammai.

On the negative side, however, the quest for spiritual fulfillment by females to meet their own needs lacked the encouragement of prevailing religious orthodoxy. An ancient Jewish prayer taught men to give thanks daily, "Blessed art thou, O Lord our God, who hast not made me a woman."[7] As if that were not bad enough, this followed two previous blessings in which the male thanked God because he had "not made me a Gentile or a slave." Montefiore dares to draw the conclusion: "'Women, children and slaves': that familiar and frequent collocation means and reveals a great deal. Women were, on the whole, regarded as inferior to men in mind, in function, and in status."[8] At times this attitude became open contempt: "Happy is he whose children are males, and woe to him whose children are females" (b*Qid.* 82b). Josephus summarized the popular understanding of his time: "The woman, says the Law, is in all things inferior to the man. Let her accordingly be submissive, not for her humiliation, but

---

[7]For details of this blessing both in the ancient Near Eastern world and in the modern Jewish prayer book see Albrecht Oepke, "*gune*," *Theological Dictionary of the New Testament*, ed. Gerhard Kittel (Grand Rapids MI: Eerdmans, 1964) 1:777 and n. 4 (hereinafter abbreviated *TDNT*).

[8]C. G. Montefiore, *A Rabbinic Anthology* (Cleveland: World Publishing, 1963 reprint), 18.

that she may be directed; for the authority has been given by God to the man."[9]

This theory of female subordination was translated consistently into religious institutional practice. At birth, girl babies did not undergo circumcision, or any other compensatory rite, despite the fact that this was the supreme mode of initiation into the Jewish commonwealth, the lifetime badge of belonging to Israel. Consider the implications of Jews styling themselves as "the Circumcised" (Eph. 2:11) when at least half of their number had not been so marked because of their anatomy determined before birth by gender!

Nor was there any possibility of women becoming priests, Levites, or rabbis, regardless of their ancestry or aptitude. This was unthinkable, in part, because of the inordinate stress placed on religious defilement as a result of such natural bodily functions as menstruation, which could render the women unclean one-fourth of the time (Lev. 15:19-30). Just as females were restricted to a small, crowded court in the Temple, so in the synagogues they were segregated, often in a balcony behind screens as mere spectators, and their presence was not counted in determining a quorum.

The sexual barrier in the Temple stood, therefore, as a visible expression of a centuries-old assumption within Judaism that it was a male responsibility to negotiate the divine-human relationship and that it was a female responsibility to follow the path to God marked out by the dominant man in her life. Since virtually all of our ancient sources have masculine authors, there is no way to estimate,

---

[9]Josephus, *Against Apion* 2.201. The passage was textually suspect to Niese (because of possible Christian influence!) but it accords with the tenor of this entire section (24) on marriage laws.

at this distance, how much hostility was engendered by this inherently unequal system. Suffice it to say that, as long as the barrier existed, women would never be able to realize their fullest spiritual potential.

III

But Paul was convinced that Christ had already broken down all such sexual walls during his earthly life and had thereby destroyed the enmity that they fostered (Ephesians 2:14). To discover the basis for the Apostle's claim we must examine the place of women in the earthly ministry of Jesus.

In proclaiming the gospel of salvation, Jesus quickly moved from the limited setting of the synagogue to the wide-open places where all might hear him without restriction (e.g. Mk. 1:32-34, 45; 3:7-10; 4:1-2). Both by word and by deed he declared that a whole new order called the kingdom of God was ready to be established. Signs of its inbreak were seen especially in the miracles, that he performed—without distinction—for women as well as men (Lk. 13:10-17; 7:11-17). By offering free and full forgiveness directly to women, Jesus was clearly inviting them to experience the blessings of the age to come on the basis of faith alone (Lk. 7:48-50).

We observed in the preceding chapter that Jesus' emphasis on faith instead of circumcision as the basis of one's standing before God had the effect of placing Jew and Gentile alike on equal religious footing. But it is just as obvious that this shift from hereditary privilege to personal commitment had the same equalizing effect on religious opportunities available to male and female. For faith, unlike circumcision, by its very nature is no respecter of gender. Moreover, because faith is indifferent to biological distinctions rooted in birth, it offers no support to the sexual taboos on which the Jewish system of female defilement was built. The woman with an issue of blood, for example, was, by her unmentionable malady, rendered so ceremonially unclean that she could not even touch Jesus (Lev. 15:25-27). Yet she could reach out to him with as much faith as any man, and it was such faith that brought her a full measure of bodily healing and inner peace (Mk. 5:25-34).

Such openness to, and trust in, the powers of the New Age operating through the ministry of Jesus inescapably involved an element of individual decision. Nor did Jesus shrink from spelling out the possible consequences. Women were to make their own religious commitment to him even if it shattered the solidarity of the family circle (Matt. 10:35; Lk. 12:53). Here we must remember that the Mosaic code gave the father of an unmarried woman or the husband of a married woman "the right to affirm or to annul any vow or promise that she has made" (Num. 30:13 TEV).

It was unthinkable in Judaism to demand, as Jesus did, that mother and daughter choose for or against him even if this divided their own home. Such a radical claim shows that the liberation that Jesus offered to women was at once both judgment and mercy, that is, liberation *for* unfettered discipleship in the family of faith, as well as liberation *from* traditional security in the family of flesh.

Many women did make that hard but glad choice because, through Jesus, the transforming reign of God had come into their lives. Luke 8:2 tells us that "some women who had been healed of evil spirits and diseases" (TEV) followed him, together with the twelve disciples, from the time of the Galilean ministry. Three of them are named (Mary Magdalene, Joanna, Susanna), presumably because they were well known in the early church, in addition to "many other women who used their own resources to help Jesus and his disciples" (Lk 8:3 TEV).

The compelling power of his call was such that these women from Galilee were the last at the cross in courage (Matt. 27:55-56), the first at the tomb in love (Mk. 16:1). But the truly incredible fact is not that women so completely outperformed men in this last great showdown, but rather that they were so directly involved in these climactic events at all. "The fact that women followed Jesus is without precedent in contemporary Judaism."[10]

It is important to grasp the theological reality underlying this remarkable pattern. Albrecht Oepke provides a clue: "Jesus is not the radical reformer who proclaims laws and seeks to enforce a transformation of relationships. He is the Savior who gives Himself especially to the lowly and oppressed and calls all without distinction to the freedom of the Kingdom of God."[11]

So decisive was this breakthrough that it quickly took root in the early church, even though Christianity had emerged from the womb of Judaism. Women shared together with men in preparation for Pentecost (Acts 1:14) and were the direct recipients of its spiritual blessings (Acts 2:16-18). A woman's home became the earliest known house-church in

---

[10]Werner Foerster, *Palestinian Judaism in New Testament Times* (Edinburgh: Oliver & Boyd, 1964) 127. This does not imply that Jewish women had no contact with rabbis or expressed no interest in their teachings. The reference here is to women who attended Jesus as a vocation throughout his Galilean and Judean ministry.

[11]Oepke, *TDNT* 1:784.

Jerusalem (Acts 12:12). At Philippi, women founded a new congregation under the leadership of Lydia (Acts 16:13-15). Both Jewish and Greek women of high standing were among the first to be converted (Acts 17:4, 12, 34). In some cases of ministry by a couple, the wife was mentioned in pride of place before her husband, as with Priscilla and Aquila (Acts 18:26; Rom. 16:3), presumably because of her more outstanding Christian leadership.

The earliest pattern of church organization was obviously fluid, but even at this first stage women began to emerge in a variety of both functional and formal roles. Priscilla was a "fellow-worker" (Romans 16:3), one of Paul's most endearing terms for his closest colleagues in ministry. Phoebe was a "deacon" or servant of the church at Cenchreae (Romans 16:1). Philip's four unmarried daughters were "prophetesses" in Caesarea (Acts 21:9). As the church developed, a somewhat official order of mature women "presbyters" seems to have emerged to deal especially with the problems of widows (1 Tim. 5:3-16; Titus 2:3-5).

Both the frequency with which women were mentioned, often without reference to their husbands, as well as the prominence of their roles, provide abundant testimony to the new freedom which was theirs in Christ (Acts 9:36; Rom. 16:6, 12, 15; 1 Cor. 1:11; 9:5; Col. 4:15; Phil. 4:2-3; Philem. 2). Whatever position they might hold, one key contention was that it be "*likewise*" with positions held by men (1 Tim. 3:11, in comparison with vv. 1 and 8).

It is sometimes supposed that Paul was not sympathetic to sexual equality within the church because he enjoined women to silence in 1 Timothy 2:11-12 (cf. 1 Cor. 14:34-35). A careful consideration of such passages suggests that the Apostle may have been combating spiritual enthusiasts who made immature female converts so intoxicated with their sense of Christian freedom that they were misusing their newly discovered opportunities for religious fulfillment. Because the church was so far ahead of the world in its attitude toward women, Paul cautioned them to be circumspect, lest *outsiders* misunderstand their boldness. However, even in the unstable church at Corinth, he conceded that the role of women to *insiders* included praying and prophesying in public worship (1 Cor. 11:5), a responsibility that they could hardly discharge without speaking both to and for the congregation as spiritual leaders![12]

For Paul, however, regardless of the historical circumstances with which he was forced to deal in struggling young churches, the ultimate theological principle was never in doubt. Not only did he approach the social barrier by affirming that in Christ there is "no longer Jew nor Greek." He also approached the sexual barrier with a parallel affirmation: "There is no longer male and female; for all of you are one in Christ Jesus" (Gal. 3:28). This was not merely a claim that in Christ the "male and female" duality of creation had been redeemed from its corruption by sin but also that in

[12]The point may be that women in the congregation were not to be disruptive by speaking out while the service was in progress. Jean Héring, *The First Epistle of Saint Paul to the Corinthians* (London: Epworth Press, 1962) 154, comments: "So there is a clear distinction between a preaching woman (using the term in its widest sense), who has the right to bring a message—and a woman who is merely present at worship as an ordinary member of the congregation. The latter should be silent." The same, of course, would apply to men as well. On the possible tension between Paul and spiritual enthusiasts over the role of women, see James E. Crouch, *The Origin and Intention of the Colossian Haustafel* (Göttingen: Vandenhoeck & Ruprecht, 1972) 131-44.

the life of the Body of Christ (v. 27) it had actually been transcended.[13] Those who live by a faith (v. 26) which expresses itself in baptism (v. 27a), have thereby been "clothed" with a Christ-identity (v. 27b) which supersedes both social and sexual identities.

Once again, let us give credit to Judaism where credit is due. This religion had gone a long way toward elevating the dignity of woman, strengthening the sanctity of her sex and the stability of her home life. As with heredity, the Christian difference was one of degree. Because we do not determine either the family ancestry or the sexual identity to which one is born, it is not for us arbitrarily to assign priorities and preferences to factors over which we have no control. Not only by creation but, as our primary passage indicates (Eph. 2:13), by the cross ("blood") of Christ are such distinctions abolished. Standing at Calvary, neither genealogy nor gender matters in the approach to God.

IV

To be sure, some Christian groups have made modest progress toward the religious emancipation of woman. A typical Christian church today, particularly in urban areas of the Western world, finds both sexes seated together, often in

---

[13]Krister Stendahl, *The Bible and the Role of Women* (Philadelphia: Fortress Press, 1966) 32, points out that Paul interrupted his "neither/nor" series in v. 28 in order to quote the actual phrase from Genesis 1:27, "male *and* female" so as to suggest that "the most primary division of God's creation is overcome, that between *male* and *female*—the terminology points... in the direction of man as the image of God, beyond the division into male and female."

family units, for worship. In most communions, women feel free to make independent religious decisions, such as for church membership, without being bound to the faith (or nonfaith) of the dominant male in their family. Women are welcome to sing in the choir, accept volunteer assignments in the educational program particularly involving children, and even fill a few professional positions on the church staff. Qualified women have long served magnificently as career missionaries and in mainline denominations are gaining increased access to other leadership roles traditionally reserved for men. Clearly we have *lowered* the sexual barrier, but have we *leveled* it to the ground?

In response to that question it must be admitted that Christianity, again like ancient Judaism, is still a man's world, particularly in the Roman Catholic Church and in those Evangelical congregations influenced by fundamentalism. Even in many Protestant churches women give as much as half or more of the money, yet financial responsibilities are almost exclusively a male domain. Often females comprise well over half the members of a congregation but lack any representation on its "official board," such as the diaconate. For some reason, ordination—even though a minor feature of ministry in the New Testament—is fiercely guarded in many churches, and even in whole denominations, as a male prerogative. The power structure of most boards that control religious institutions is basically one-sided; even agencies with major responsibilities to female employees and/or clients often have few or no women either as trustees or as executive officers, even though women have proved their ability to lead some of the largest corporations in the world. It cannot be denied that women have won a greater measure of political equality as American citizens than they have won religious equality as "citizens with the saints and also members of the household of God" (Ephesians 2:19).

The crux of the problem lies just here. In the New Testament era, under the liberating impact of the ministry of Jesus, the church surged far *ahead* of its world in the freedom which it extended to women to find fulfillment in Christ. But in the present era, under the dead weight of unexamined tradition, the church now lags far *behind* the world in the same regard. Wide support is given to those who champion a theology of "subjection" or "subordination" on the basis of such passages as, "Wives submit yourselves unto your own husbands, as unto the Lord" (Eph. 5:22 KJV). This glaring misinterpretation was demolished years ago by W. O. Carver, a careful and profound student of Ephesians, who pointed out:

> There is no imperative form in the Greek. The word does not mean obey. Furthermore, the voice of the participle is not active or passive, but middle. It carries an exhortation to women in the disposal of their own lives.... This perversion of grammar, syntax and sense has become "law" instead of gospel and has found place in the approved marriage ceremony of the sacramental churches from which most of the democratic churches have borrowed it.[14]

In case that explanation is a bit technical for some readers, the point is that Ephesians 5:22 has a subject ("the

---

[14]W. O. Carver, *The Glory of God in the Christian Calling* (Nashville: Broadman Press, 1949) 168, with further comment on this passage on 165-69. The section quoted in the text also appears in *Review and Expositor* 38 (1941): 256.

women") but no verb because it is only one application of the preceding verse 21 where *all* Christians, both male and female alike, are encouraged not to dominate relationships by insisting on their own rights but rather are to "subject" their wills to one another "in the sense of voluntary yielding in love."[15]

One other passage has been given undue prominence and distorted application by those determined to keep women behind a sexual barrier, the twofold insistence in 1 Timothy 3:2, 12 that church leaders (bishops, deacons) must be the "husband of one wife." Applied literally and legalistically, even to men, this qualification would have excluded John the Baptist, Jesus, and Paul, even as today it would exclude single men, widowed men, and remarried men. But to interpret it as meaning that women should never be church leaders because that right is reserved for their husbands completely disenfranchises all of those women who have no male spiritual "head" because they are single, widowed, or married to a non-Christian. The New Testament, taken as a whole, does not support the edifice of male chauvinism which some have tried to erect upon it.

Despite the achievement of equality by women in almost every other area of life, many Christians still debate whether they should also be accorded religious equality, particularly as regards the ministerial offices of pastor and deacon. What this sometimes acrimonious discussion overlooks is the unambiguous teaching of the New Testament that *all* Christians constitute a priesthood, which means that every

---

[15]Walter Bauer and others, *A Greek-English Lexicon of the New Testament and Other Early Christian Literature,* 2nd ed. (Chicago: University of Chicago Press, 1979) 848. The third edition does not retain this felicitous rendering.

woman believer is to be a priest! Bear in mind that this is the most historic, the most exalted, and the most frequently used term for ministerial office in the Bible. The situation in the early Christian movement was so fluid that we may never be able to determine with finality all of the specific roles in which women regularly functioned. But we do know for certain that all of them functioned as priests (1 Pet. 2:5, 9; Rev. 1:6; 5:10).

The central issue that we face today is not whether we will deny a few of our women their desire for the diaconate or the pastorate but whether we will deny *all* of our women their God-given priesthood! If we boldly implement the priesthood of *every* believer for male and female alike in all of its biblical richness, then our fruitless bickering over the use of women in this or that particular place of service will solve itself. If by faith every woman is divinely appointed to the royal priesthood of the New Israel, then God has already answered the question of whether we may set apart gifted women to any position of service for which they are qualified.

Many sincere Christians are afraid of this emphasis because it seems to imply sympathy and support for the militant feminist movement that marches under the banner of "Women's Lib." Clearly there is a radical wing of the "new sisterhood" with its roots in assumptions foreign to biblical faith. But there is no need to endorse or even identify with this secular expression of the struggle for women's rights in order to implement the Christ-centered teachings of the New Testament. Our concern is not so much with legal rights as with spiritual responsibilities. If God does, in fact, give spiritual gifts to women, which has been unmistakably clear since Pentecost, then the crucial task of the church is to cultivate such gifts and to provide a channel for their effective expression.

The deepest tragedy of building sexual barriers is that it forces the church to utilize only half of its available resources in attempting to fulfill its mission. In a day when religious indifference threatens the retreat of Christianity as a potent force in contemporary life, it is foolish to fight God's battles with one hand tied behind us by ignoring or even suppressing the contribution of half our forces. The important thing at this stage in the church's struggle for spiritual equality is not for men to debate whether women be *allowed* to enter certain areas hitherto open only to males, but to create a climate in which it simply *does not matter* whether one is male or female but only whether one has a gift from God to offer the Body of Christ.

The apocryphal *Gospel of Thomas* discovered at Nag Hammadi, Egypt, in 1945 concludes with a request attributed to Simon Peter, "Let Mary leave us, for women are not worthy of life." To this shocking suggestion the tractate makes Jesus reply, "I myself shall lead her in order to make her male, so that she too may become a living spirit resembling you males. For every woman who will make herself male will enter the Kingdom of Heaven" (saying 114).[16] The time has come to repudiate this Gnostic heresy in the contemporary church by removing every restriction that would require a woman to become a man in order to qualify for full participation. Christians must never forget that the

---

[16]James M. Robinson, ed., *The Nag Hammadi Library* (New York: Harper & Row, 1977) 130.

truly *new* birth which Christ brings represents a shift from flesh to spirit, not from female to male (Jn. 3:6)!

Since it is often charged that the emphasis in this chapter is somehow an excursion into recent liberal ideology rather than the recovery of an ancient biblical conviction, let me close with words from a conservative Bible encyclopedia written nearly a century ago regarding the future of woman from a scriptural perspective:

> The freedom wherewith Christ did set us free includes [woman's] complete liberation to equality of opportunity with man. In mental endowment, in practical ability, in all the higher ministries of life and even in statecraft, she has proved herself the equal of man. Christianity always tends to place woman side by side with man in all the great achievements of education, art, literature, the humanities, social service, and missions. The entire movement of modern society toward her perfect enfranchisement is the distinct and inevitable product of the teaching of Jesus.... The result of this latest evolution of Christianity will not only be a new womanhood for the race but, through her enlightenment, culture and spiritual leadership, a new humanity.[17]

---

[17]Dwight M. Pratt, "Woman," *The International Standard Bible Encyclopedia*, James Orr, ed. (Grand Rapids MI: Eerdmans, 1939 reprint) 5:3104.

4

Beyond the Sacral Barrier

I

Temple worshipers able to move beyond both the social barrier, separating Gentile from Jew, and the sexual barrier, separating female from male, would find themselves standing before a semicircular staircase of fifteen steps at the western end of the Court of Women.[1] Here the Levites gathered to play musical instruments and to sing, especially the "Songs of Ascents," or fifteen "Psalms of the Steps" (Ps. 120-34), during the Feast of Tabernacles (Mishnah, *Sukkah* 5.4; *Middoth* 2.5).

Climbing to the top of this eleven-foot rise, one entered the most impressive gate in the entire Temple complex, called the Corinthian Gate in Josephus, Nicanor's Gate in the Mishnah, and the Beautiful Gate in the New Testament.[2] It

---

[1]Descriptions of the inner court are found in Josephus, *Jewish War* 5.226; *Jewish Antiquities* 15.419; and in the Mishnah, *Middoth* 2.5-6; 5.1.

[2]There is some difficulty in utilizing the ancient sources to make a precise identification of this gate, due primarily to obscurity in the language of Josephus when describing the main gates on the eastern and western sides of the Court of Women. For a full discussion see F. J. Hollis, *The Archaeology of Herod's Temple, with a Commentary on the Tractate "Middoth"* (London: J. M. Dent, 1934) 167-88. On the Corinthian or Bronze Gate in Josephus see *Jewish War* 2.411; 5.201, 204-206; *Jewish Antiquities* 15.418. On the Nicanor Gate in the Mishnah see *Shekalim* 6.3; *Yoma* 6.3; *Sotah*

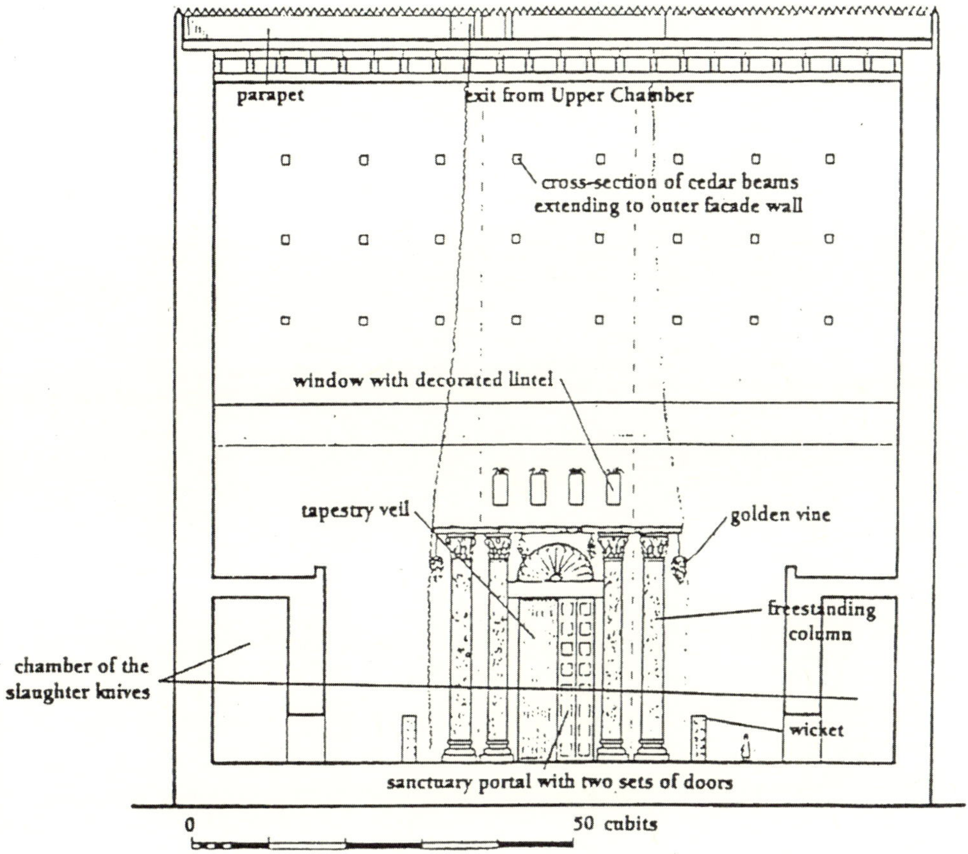

The Facade of the Sanctuary

stood seventy-five feet high with double wicket doors, each sixty feet wide, thus being much larger than the other nine gates to the sacred enclosure which were only forty-five feet in height with double doors each twenty-two and one-half feet in width. This great portal was so termed by Josephus because it was made of Corinthian bronze, famous for its beauty and value. It was more richly ornamented than the others, being overlaid with plates of silver and gold so massive that at least twenty men were needed to close it (Josephus, *Jewish War* 6.293).

The Nicanor Gate was honored above all others because it provided access to the Temple proper, the Holy Place where everything to be done "before the Lord," that is, in the service of worship, was performed.[3] This inner court was itself divided into two parts. The first section reached after passing through the gate was the Court of Israel, sometimes called the Court of Men because it could be entered by Jewish males but not females.[4] This area lay against the edges of the

---

1.5; *Middoth* 1.4; 2.3, 6; *Negaim* 14.8. On the Beautiful Gate in the New Testament see Acts 3:2, 10.

[3]The consecrated area to which the Nicanor Gate led was called "sacred" (*ha-mikdosh*) by the Jews. At first this was translated into Greek as to *hagion*, but gradually the Greek term *to hieron*, which had elsewhere been applied to pagan cults, came also to be used, as in Josephus, *Jewish Antiquities* 15.419. For details see Elias J. Bickerman, "The Warning Inscriptions of Herod's Temple," *The Jewish Quarterly Review* n.s. 37 (1946—1947): 388-89. In the New Testament, the usage of *to hieron* was extended to cover the whole Temple precinct, as in Mark 11:11, 15.

[4]Although Josephus indicates that women were completely excluded from the inner court, as discussed in the preceding chapter, in the pre-Herodian era they may have been allowed access to offer sacrifice for themselves. Details in Gustaf Dalman, *Sacred Sites and Ways* (London:

sacred enclosure just inside the surrounding wall. According to the Mishnah, it comprised a narrow strip only sixteen and one-half feet wide which ran along the 202 and one-half-foot eastern border of the inner court somewhat like a vestibule (*Middoth* 5.1). Josephus, however, implies that this sixteen-and-a-half-foot strip surrounded the Sanctuary on all sides (*Jewish Antiquities* 8.95; 13.373; *Jewish War* 5.226), which would mean that it turned westward on both the north and the south to form a U-shape around the second or innermost section of the Holy Place called the Court of Priests, so named because it was restricted to the authorized priesthood of Israel.

As in every other part of the Temple which we have thus far visited, there was also a barrier here separating these two courts. Josephus described it in accordance with his understanding of the layout of the Temple as follows: "Surrounding both the sanctuary and the altar was a low stone parapet, fair and graceful, about a cubit high, which separated the laity outside from the priests" (*Jewish War* 5.226). The Mishnah, on the other hand, consistent with its view of the Court of Israel as an outer vestibule, envisioned the divider as a step made by turning up the ends of flagstones, but agreed with Josephus that it stood one cubit (eighteen inches) high. On top of this elevation rested a platform constructed of three additional steps, on which the Levites sang a daily psalm. Since each of these risers was nine inches tall, all of the gradations together made the Court of Priests forty-five inches higher than the Court of Israel (*Middoth* 2.6).

S.P.C.K., 1935) 298n.4; Joachim Jeremias, *Jerusalem in the Time of Jesus* (London: SCM Press, 1969) 373n.74.

This architectural separation and elevation was intended to symbolize a theological distinction between laity and clergy in the religion of Judaism. Temple arrangements reinforced a rationale that understood priests as inherently more holy than other people. Because of this, they were uniquely authorized to exercise a representative function on the people's behalf in relation to God as well as a representative function on behalf of God in relation to the people. The technical name for this underlying assumption is sacerdotalism, a doctrinal viewpoint that legitimizes a special class of cultic officials as mediators between the human and the divine. Here, then, in our third Temple area, we are faced with what we may call the *sacral* barrier between clergy and laity. Let us now attempt to discern some of the implications of its function.

II

Judaism in the time of Jesus and Paul was a profoundly sacerdotal religion in the sense just described. Since its priests were to embody the holiness of the covenant people and to serve God in his own House, their selection obviously could not be made on the basis of human merit, such as religious interest or theological training. Instead, selection was by ancestry, the male offspring of priestly families qualifying for this vocation by virtue of a birth over which they had no control. Although a hereditary priesthood did have the advantage of a certain impartiality, this arbitrary principle of selection admitted to its ranks many who were manifestly unsuited for such service. As we shall see, the resulting cleavage between formal suitability and functional unsuitability for the priesthood was to become a source of tension particularly during the Hasmonean and Herodian periods leading up to the New Testament era.

In order to insure as pure a bloodline as possible, hereditary qualifications became increasingly selective as the centuries passed. The earliest Israelite priesthood was to include all of the descendants of Levi, one of the twelve patriarchs of Israel. But by the time of the monarchy it had come to be limited to the descendants of only one prominent Levite, namely Aaron. Then, by the time of the exile, Ezekiel, in particular, championed only the descendants of a priest in the time of David named Zadok, which would have restricted the legitimate lineage even further. We know from the Dead Sea Scrolls discovered at Qumran in 1947 that a keen interest in priestly descent continued into the New Testament period and was a source of bitter hostility within Jewish sectarian movements at the very time when Paul wrote of a "dividing wall of hostility" in Ephesians 2:14.

The practical effect of these complex power struggles, which were precipitated primarily by the ever-increasing centralization of worship in Jerusalem, was to proliferate a priestly hierarchy in which the heirs of the victors came to be ranked in power and prestige above the heirs of the vanquished. By the time of the Herodian Temple, an elaborate bureaucracy had emerged which we can sketch here only in bare outline.[5]

---

[5]One of the more informative summaries of the first-century Jewish priesthood is by Jeremias, *Jerusalem in the Time of Jesus,* 147-213. This treatment concludes with a detailed survey of hereditary requirements for priestly marriages, 213-21. Another helpful survey is Emil Schürer, *The History of the Jewish People in the Age of Jesus Christ,* new English version rev.

1. At the lowest level were the Levites, an inferior clergy descended from those preexilic priests deposed by the Deuteronomic reform. As the name implied, they were broadly considered as descendants of the patriarch Levi but not from the more prestigious line running through Aaron. Because of their subordinate status, they took no part in the sacrificial system, being limited solely to the performance of Temple music and a variety of menial tasks such as custodial and police work. Illustrative of their limited sanctity was the prohibition on pain of death from approaching the altar or entering the Sanctuary building (Num. 18:3).

2. At the heart of the system were the ordinary priests who offered sacrifices and tended the showbread, incense, and candelabra in the Holy Place of the Sanctuary. All of these regular priests traced their genealogy back to Aaron and were married to wives descended from priests, Levites, or purebred Israelites. They were organized into twenty-four "courses" or administrative units that served at the Temple in rotation for two weeks each year plus the three great festivals (Lk. 1:5-10). During the remaining eleven months of the year they lived at home, many of them in the hill country of Judea, where they pursued other vocations, usually manual, and assisted occasionally in the administration of the religious law (Mk. 1:44).

3. At the top of this hierarchical pyramid was the priestly aristocracy of Jerusalem that originally was rooted in the Zadokite lineage. From this close-knit clan came the leading Temple officers, collectively referred to as "chief priests,"

---

and ed. by Geza Vermes, Fergus Millar, and Matthew Black (Edinburgh: T. & T. Clark, 1979) 2:223-91.

including the captain of the Temple, the directors of the twenty-four weekly courses of priests, the overseers, and the treasurers (Acts 4:1, 5-6). At the apex of this summit was the one high priest who held, supposedly for life, the most important office not only in the Temple but, without a king, in the nation as well. Symbolic of his primacy was the privilege of being the only person authorized to enter the Holy of Holies, that innermost recess in the Sanctuary building which otherwise remained empty because there the presence of God was concentrated as at no other place on earth. This he did only on the Day of Atonement in order to sprinkle blood for the purification of the Sanctuary and the forgiveness of the sins of the people not covered by the regular sacrifices (Lev. 16; Mishnah, *Yoma* 5.1-4; *Kelim* 1.9; *Tamid* 3.8).

It does not take much historical imagination to realize that a system based so exclusively on bloodline was shot through with nepotism, manipulated marriages, and family intrigue. Moreover, the rigid stratification of the priesthood into competing social classes intensified the natural jealousies which always seemed to fester between wealthy urban elites and poorer rural pietists.

Compounding all of these inherent structural difficulties was a troubled history of political intervention from the time of the Seleucids to the fall of Jerusalem (175 BC to AD 70) which resulted in a succession of illegitimate high priests being installed in office, replacing legitimate Zadokite high priests. This melancholy legacy of treachery, murder, usurpation, and defiance deeply compromised the credibility of the priesthood and enraged the populace who had no effective control over its own clergy (Josephus, *Jewish Antiquities* 20.179-81, 205-207).

One vivid illustration of this corruption may be cited because of its bearing on our theme of Temple barriers. From 103 to 76 BC, Alexander Jannaeus occupied the high priesthood by inheritance as a member of the Hasmonean dynasty, despite the fact that this family belonged to the ordinary priestly clan of Joiarib instead of to the deposed Oniads (named Onias) who were lawful successors to the Zadokites. Because the Joiarib clan had not returned to Palestine until long after the Exile, it did not deserve full membership in a regular priestly division, much less the high priesthood itself. Moreover, Alexander's grandmother, wife of the high priest Simon, had been taken captive under Antiochus IV, thereby rendering her descendants illegitimate priests because female prisoners of war were viewed as deflorated women, whether abused by their captors or not, and so placed on the level of prostitutes (Josephus, *Against Apion* 1.35; *Jewish Antiquities* 3.276; 13.292). To make matters worse, Alexander began his high priesthood by marrying Salome, widow of his deceased brother Aristobulus who had preceded him as king, which was a gross violation of the levitical law that a priest should marry only a virgin (Lev. 21:13-14).[6]

Here, then, was a lusty warrior king, who enjoyed nothing more than wild battles and even wilder parties, officiating at the altar of God! Openly contemptuous of the ceremonial regulations which the Pharisees venerated as divine law, Alexander Jannaeus finally goaded the citizenry into rebellion in the very courts of the Temple. At the

---

[6]For the details of Jewish law that rendered Alexander Jannaeus an illegitimate high priest, see Jeremias, *Jerusalem in the Time of Jesus*, 154-56, 188-89, 216-21.

morning liturgy held during the Feast of Tabernacles, it was customary for each worshiper to carry a palm branch (the *lulab*) in the right hand and citrus fruit (the *ethrog*) in the left hand. On one such occasion, the worshipers became so incensed over the careless way that Alexander spilled the water-libation over his feet onto the ground instead of carefully pouring it into the correct bowl on the altar[7] that, as Josephus describes it,

> they pelted him with citrons... and they added insult to injury by saying that he was descended from captives and was unfit to hold office and to sacrifice; and being enraged at this, he killed some six thousand of them, and also placed a wooden barrier around the altar and the Temple as far as the coping (of the court) which the priests alone were permitted to enter, and by this means blocked the people's way to him. (*Jewish Antiquities* 13.372-73)

This temporary barricade, bristling with hostility, represented not only a restoration of the permanent parapet that had stood in the Solomonic Temple (Josephus, *Jewish Antiquities* 8.95) but was also a harbinger of the fixed divider that was built into the Herodian Temple. In light of the circumstances prompting its erection by Alexander Jannaeus, it is the height of irony—a triumph of theory over reality!—that sacerdotal theology legitimated such a wall on the

---

[7]This specific provocation is not reported by Josephus but appears in the rabbinic literature in reference to an unnamed high priest who is usually identified with Alexander Jannaeus because of the similarity of the incident (Mishnah, *Sukkah* 4.9).

grounds that it protected a "holy" priesthood from profanation by ordinary laymen.

But there was yet a deeper flaw in the wall than this institutionalization of hypocrisy that, so to speak, set corruption in concrete. Perhaps the most serious indictment that could be leveled against this wall was that it fostered a proxy relationship with God.

To be sure, ideally the priests officiated as representatives of the lay people who were forbidden to do the work of clergy. Yet in facilitating a divine-human encounter there are inherent limitations to the efficacy of one person acting for another. Legal relationships may be negotiated by an authorized agent because the desired result is a formal contract, but religious relationships do not permit such a substitution because the desired result is intimate communion. In some states, for example, marriages may be celebrated by proxy but they cannot be consummated by proxy! Just so, the elaborate liturgical actions of the priesthood dramatized, on center stage as it were, the terms of Israel's historical covenant with God. But that pageantry, for all its impressiveness, left those who beheld it as spectators standing behind a rail, detached from personal participation in the cosmic drama to which it pointed.

III

For Paul, a temple without walls of hostility meant that Christ had also broken down the sacerdotal barrier between clergy and laity. To determine how that happened, let us take another look at the ministry of Jesus. It began with the work of a forerunner, John the Baptist, who by virtue of ancestry (Lk. 1:5) had both the vocational opportunity and sacred obligation to follow his father in becoming a priest. The fact that John's career took a radically different turn may mean that he deliberately renounced the official priesthood as corrupt and, like the community at Qumran, turned to the wilderness with a message of judgment on the temple system.[8] This would explain both his denunciation of the priestly aristocracy as a "brood of vipers" proud of their ancestry, and his conviction that God could use humble desert stones to raise up a temple formed by true sons of Abraham who would worship him more genuinely than those who stood amid the fine stones of the Jerusalem Temple (Mt. 3:7-10).[9]

By seeking baptism at the hands of John, Jesus voluntarily associated himself from the outset with one whose whole ministry was a repudiation of Jewish sacerdotalism. It is significant that, near the end of his own ministry, when challenged to identify the authority by which he had condemned the Jerusalem Temple, Jesus harked back to the example of his predecessor (Mk. 11:27-33). For neither man had the authority of ordination or of office: John because he had elected not to enter the priesthood, Jesus because he had received no rabbinic training or certification. Each had clearly *functioned* as a minister, yet both had the *formal* status of laymen. The correct answer to the recurring question, "By what authority . . .?" was the same for Jesus as for John: *their authority was from God!* They were commissioned directly

---

[8]This interpretation was advanced, even before the Dead Sea Scrolls could be utilized, by Carl H. Kraeling, *John the Baptist* (New York: Charles Scribner's Sons, 1951) 24-26.

[9]Kraeling, *John the Baptist*, 48-51.

from heaven (Mk. 1:11) and depended entirely on God to authenticate their ministries in the lives of others (Matt. 11:7-11, 18-19, 25-27).

Not only was Jesus a layman, but he gathered about himself a company of twelve followers who were laymen as well. Ancestry obviously mattered not at all in their selection. No attention was given to the genealogy of their wives, or to physical defects, or to purificatory rites, or to proper vestments, or to any of the other qualifications about which we read so much in the Jewish literature. From what little we know about the background of the Twelve, it is safe to say that in every respect they were the antithesis of a company of priests. Their training was entirely personal and relational, never institutional or ceremonial. When sent out on mission, they were to depend entirely on spontaneous response to direct encounter (Mark 6:11-12). Even though they symbolized the nucleus of the reconstituted twelve tribes of Israel for the New Age (Matt. 19:28), no provision was made for a "holy" tribe such as the Levites. From all the evidence it is clear that sacerdotalism was simply not operative in the mind and ministry of Jesus.

That foundational fact goes far toward explaining the complete transformation of the priestly role in the early church. The Hebrew word for priest (*kohen*) occurs more than 700 times in the Old Testament, usually of cultic officials, whereas its Greek counterpart (*hiereus*) appears only thirty-one times in the New Testament, never of a Christian ministerial office. Instead, its only application there as a Christian concept is to the entire church, rather than to a select group within the people of God. J. A. T. Robinson has commented aptly on the dramatic change:

> Yet surely one of the most remarkable facts in the history of religion is the astonishing and well-nigh total eclipse in the New Testament of the priestly side of the Old Testament religion.... The whole elaborate liturgy of the Temple and the sacrificial system which lay at the very centre of Jewish religion was given up with extraordinarily little heart searching.... The *un*priestly character of early Christianity must surely have been one of the first things to strike an outsider, whether he were Jew or pagan.[10]

This does not mean, however, that the early church rejected the priesthood out of an anticlerical bias so as to become an exclusively lay movement. On the contrary, it did just the opposite by applying the priestly vocation to *every* believer (1 Pet. 2:5, 9; Rev. 1:5-6; 5:9-10; 20:6), as had been done of Israel in Exodus 19:6 and Isaiah 61:6.

Terms that had once been used to describe the formal rituals performed by priests were now spiritualized and applied to every aspect of Christian living. Paul, for example, likened his whole "ministry" (Greek *leitourgon,* from which we derive "liturgy") to a "priesting" (Greek *hierourgounta*) of the gospel in which he presented to God "offerings" (Greek *prosphora*) consisting not of animals but of Gentiles converted by his labors and made "holy" (Greek *hegiasemene*) by the Holy Spirit (Rom. 15:16). Unlike Jewish worshipers who stood back and watched as the priest offered an animal sacrifice on the altar, Paul urged Christians to present themselves "as a

---

[10]J. A. T. Robinson, *On Being the Church in the World* (London: SCM Press, 1960) 72.

living sacrifice" (Rom. 12:1) and so to combine in their service of Christ the role of the priest with that of the offering (Phil. 2:17, 24, 30; 4:18; 2 Cor. 2:15).

This uniting—and, hence, transcending—of lay and clergy roles in the early church took place in a context of thought that reinterpreted the whole cultic ideology of Israel. Since all Christians were now viewed as a "priesthood of believers" offering *themselves* in service, this meant that sacrifice had become both "living" and "spiritual" (Rom. 12:1; 1 Pet. 2:5). That being true at the altar, the sanctuary itself was seen as a building "not made with hands" by humans out of stones (Mk. 14:58; Acts 7:48), but made by God out of human lives (1 Cor. 3:16-17; 2 Cor. 6:16; Eph. 2:19-22). Indeed, the entire Holy City came to be viewed as a spiritual reality in the heavens rather than as a geographical reality here on earth (Gal. 4:25-26; Heb. 12:22; Rev. 3:12; 21:2, 10).

This mode of thought fulfilled the sacerdotal impulse by suffusing it throughout the common life of a people who based their identity, security, and destiny not on heredity, ordination, or office, but on personal attachment to Jesus Christ, the one High Priest who alone was worthy to mediate between God and them (Heb. 4:14–10:25).

Before attempting to leap from the first century to the twenty-first, let us observe once again that the difference between Judaism and Christianity, this time at the point of lay-clergy relations, was one of degree rather than of kind. Judaism sponsored robust lay movements during the New Testament era, of which Pharisaism was a prime example. The way in which Judaism survived the destruction of its Temple and the collapse of its priesthood in AD 70 provides abundant proof that sacerdotalism was not essential to its functioning as a religious system. But Christianity gave this dimension of lay leadership a new scope and intensity which it had not known in Judaism. Acting not out of historical necessity as in the case of the parent faith, but out of eschatological opportunity, it dismantled every vestige of hierarchical authority and abolished every thought of hereditary privilege. If we are to capture the central thrust of our New Testament legacy, we shall have to discover that same radical boldness to fulfill everything sacerdotal through the common calling of clergy and laity alike.

IV

There is no way to apply this New Testament pattern to our day without understanding the nineteen centuries that have intervened. No sooner had the apostolic age ended than Christianity began to revert to the hierarchical priesthood which it had initially transcended. By the time of Cyprian in the mid-third century, explicit sacerdotalism had again become a fundamental premise in the understanding of ministry.

With the stabilization of the Roman Catholic Church, which was to dominate Western Christendom for more than a millennium, there emerged almost exact equivalents to the Jewish system of inferior clergy (Levites/Brothers), ordinary clergy (village priests/diocesan priests), superior clergy (chief priests/bishops), and primate (high priest/pope). An essential difference, of course, was that the Jewish priesthood was hereditary whereas the Catholic priesthood, being celibate, was not. However, even here there was a partial parallel in the tendency of Catholic priests to come from certain devout families and for the pope, until quite recently, to be an Italian. Also, both systems were identical in denying the priesthood to women, although Judaism has begun to open the rabbinate to women in its Reformed branch. Modest efforts to liberalize the role of the laity have been undertaken within Roman Catholicism, but the medieval legacy remains firmly entrenched despite the impetus of Vatican II.

Efforts during the Reformation to recapture the priesthood of all believers were never entirely successful, partly because the Lutheran, Reformed, and Anglican denominations carried over in varying degrees the deeply entrenched sacerdotalism of the Catholic tradition out of which they came. Even in the Free Churches without Roman rootage, a clear doctrine and practice of lay-clergy equality has seldom been implemented except in more radical expressions such as Quakerism. Here the writings of Elton Trueblood have been notable.[11]

Today, one major cause of growing hostility between clergy and laity is the rising sense of clergy professionalism in all denominations. This new form of "guild" mentality roots, not in the traditional priestly expectation of preferment based on holy office, but in the competencies needed to minister in a modern technological society.

Consider first the revolution in ministerial training which did not become standardized until the middle of the twentieth century following World War II. Biblical study now required an intricate method of historical criticism involving linguistic, archeological, literary, and philosophical skills. Pastoral care now employed therapeutic techniques not unlike those utilized by psychoanalysts. Church admini-

---

[11]D. Elton Trueblood, *The Logic of Belief* (New York: Harper & Brothers, 1943) 79-83; *Your Other Vocation* (New York: Harper & Brothers, 1952) 13-56; *The Company of the Committed* (New York: Harper & Brothers, 1961) 24-44.

stration now drew upon management theory hitherto of concern only to upper-level business executives. Ministry became a matter of applying specialized competencies gained from three to six years of graduate-professional study in an accredited theological school. No wonder layfolk fell back in deference before this display of ministerial expertise.

A second factor prompting a new kind of clergy professionalism has arisen from the media revolution so pervasive in modern culture. Huge "electronic churches" have been spawned by the ability of radio and television ministers to reach the masses far beyond their fields of labor. Even if not intentional, these media personalities inevitably take on the characteristics of religious celebrities. Their power to influence great numbers directly via the media, *without any control by the laity*, tends to make them authoritarian leaders answerable only to a multitude of contributors whom they do not even know.

It would be foolish to minimize the influence of these media superstars by pointing out that they are relatively few in number. On the contrary, precisely because they are acting out "church" on so ubiquitous a stage do they reinforce a passive, compliant role for the laity among the millions who watch their clergy-centered approach from afar. That is why, in so many congregations, the laity, like their Jewish counterparts of old, are content to "hand over" their offering to the clergy and then stand back and watch as the minister functions in what is essentially a proxy relationship to God on their behalf.

Meanwhile, the laity feels increasingly restive with its spectator role, partly because this passivity clashes so glaringly with newer models of leadership in their workaday world and partly because they have also been gaining a lot of new technological skills that they are just as eager as clergy to use in quest for a religion that they can control. Notice how the latest developments in the media revolution help meet that need.[12]

We begin with the flood of religious books that are expected to grow faster than any other segment of the publishing industry in our generation. Digital capabilities now make it easy for anyone to self-publish a book whether they be qualified to do so or not, while e-readers such as Kindle and iPad can download almost any e-Book, whether in print or out of print, at almost any place in the world. Suddenly, in less than a decade, we have achieved unlimited access to the best and the worst ideas in print. Sorting out these endless options is not easy because books, whether electronic or print, offer an experience to be shared by one author with one reader. As such, books bypass institutions such as the church and authority figures such as its clergy. There was a time when ecclesiastical professionals had a virtual monopoly on the few religious materials available, but now, with thousands of religious books coming out each year, it is common for laypersons to tell their pastor about some provocative new title that they have read before the pastor is even aware of it.

The pace of change accelerates as we turn from verbal to visual media. The same technological breakthroughs that

---

[12]This section on the new media revolution seeks to summarize the groundbreaking work of Phyllis A. Tickle who, as early as the mid-nineties, grasped its enormous significance for the life of the church. See first her broad sketch of the religious scene, *Re-Discovering the Sacred: Spirituality in America* (New York: Crossroad, 1995); and especially its sequel, *God-Talk in America* (New York: Crossroad, 1997).

make it possible for books to be read everywhere also make it possible for television to be watched everywhere. For many viewers, the prominent electronic churches are being supplemented or even superceded by religious programming produced locally, thereby inviting the competition to enter through the front door! Laypersons often report that by flipping channels with the remote they can catch three or four preachers while eating Sunday breakfast and dressing for church. A generation ago, many churchgoers grew up knowing only the worship traditions of the denomination to which their family belonged, but now they can record, store, and study the rich diversity of almost every American religious tradition in the privacy of their home. No wonder an increasing number are joining churches based, not on denominational identity, but on musical and pulpit styles, even on the extent to which worship is presented in the entertainment format that dominates television.

The climax of this communication explosion has come with the computer and its thousands of appendages that seemingly are being invented every day. Even though these digital applications drive the ongoing transformation of both verbal and visual media, the computer is very different from written and spoken presentations, its keyboard being a standing invitation to talk back, whether to challenge, confirm, or enlarge the conversation. Boldness to speak one's mind is enhanced by the many levels of openness that may be chosen, all of the way from complete disclosure in Facebook to complete anonymity in chat rooms. Many people yearn to raise questions about religion, to express doubts about some doctrine, to urge some needed reform, or to encourage leaders to adopt new strategies, but are reluctant to do so within the church for fear of social disapproval by fellow members. The internet provides an ideal place both to argue with God and to search for human validation of one's views because it defends no theology, commends no denominational traditions, and condemns no heretics.

As such, it is a profoundly democratizing instrument. I chanced to sit at dinner one evening beside the head of higher education for women in Korea. When I asked, "What one thing is advancing opportunities for women the most in your country?," she surprised me by answering, "The computer." Then she went on to explain: "The computer is gender-blind. It knows nothing of your sex, race, age, or background unless you tell it. All that matters is the quality of the information and insight that you tap into it with the tips of your fingers." Translated to the religious sphere, the computer provides a setting in which clergy no longer wear vestments indicating rank, nor places of preferment at the head of the procession. All that matters is making sense about God to others, whether one be ordained or not. For the first time in centuries, the computer has leveled a large playing field where clergy and laity alike can address their concerns with equal candor.

This leveling process is fraught with friction between the two groups. The more that ministers view themselves as self-regulating professionals, the more they clash with laity who want a voice of their own in the determination of religious beliefs and practices. Some want a folk theology that reflects inherited convictions rather than a formal theology developed in research universities without a Christian orientation. Others want to utilize their newly available knowledge, gained by reading mediating scholars such as Marcus Borg and N. T. Wright, by watching an international group of theologians discuss cutting edge issues on DVDs, and/or by taking on-line seminary courses. In doing so, most do not want the clergy to be their gatekeepers, and the new media provides one key to unlock that door.

Now let us highlight what we have learned from this threefold probe into the communication revolution that has transformed everyone's access to the whole range of historic and contemporary theological thought.

(1) The religious life of the world is becoming far more transparent whether its guardians wish it or not. Relentless exposure by the new media means that few secrets will remain hidden in stained glass ghettos.

(2) The most striking thing about this full disclosure is its enormous diversity. After all, there are now millions of books, thousands of web sites, and hundreds of TV channels to explore. The realization that there are so many routes to the divine makes many reluctant to embrace an inherited faith-tradition without comparing it to others. In subtle ways religion becomes for them more a matter of seeking than of finding.

(3) The new media are highly individualistic, neither requiring nor encouraging any involvement with religious institutions in order to claim what they offer, most of which is free. One reads a book or works at a computer alone, while many watch television alone, particularly if they do not live with others in the home. Symbols of the total control that each person exercises over these communication transactions is the current drive to integrate all three types of media into one device that can be held in one's hand (iPad) or put in one's pocket (Android, iPhone), thereby making its provision of resources completely portable in contrast to ministerial professionals who dispense their guidance primarily in church buildings that never stray from their corner.

(4) Clergy are helpless to prevent or to control the kind of religion disseminated by the new media. Neither seminary degrees nor ordination is required for entry into this world that judges everything by audience response rather than by training or status. Institutional religion as practiced in churches and denominations is only marginally involved in the media revolution, some of its most publicized attempts to make major use of the newer technologies folding after a short time. Such difficulties are due in part to a lack of training and experience by traditional clergy but even more to deep differences between the ministerial culture and the media culture.

Now for the big picture: In the sixteenth century the Protestant Reformation introduced sweeping changes into Christendom, powerfully aided by the media revolution launched when Gutenberg's invention of the printing press put the Bible in the hands of the laity who had never owned a copy. But that reformation went only so far as leaders such as Luther and Calvin concentrated on theology and ethics, leaving issues of polity and church-state relations largely unaddressed. As a result, clergy were retained as a separate order with a defined geographical jurisdiction in which they were to function as authoritative interpreters of the Word of God and leaders of the churches. To be sure, the laity gained significant new freedoms and responsibilities as the result of this reformation, but they remained subordinate to the clergy in part because the latter were vested by the state with a number of formal powers to which the former were not entitled.

Today we have a second reformation on our hands that promises to impact Christianity as much as the first one did 500 years ago. Note how sharply the religion of the new media dominated by laity clashes with traditional religion dominated by clergy. The former is more "bottom up," the latter more "top down." The former is free of financial pressure to raise a budget from the same people year after year, while the latter often includes urgent if not desperate appeals for funds to meet growing payrolls and to maintain aging facilities. The former offers endless options from which to choose in designing a mix that best fits one's temperament, circumstances, and needs, while the latter typically offers only one standardized worship and educational format. The former is enabled by the latest technology to be so completely mobile that all of its resources are available to the individual in every situation, whereas the latter is heavily dependent on its constituency gathering in one place at one time in order to receive its resources.

The overlapping of these two fundamentally different approaches to Christianity may help to explain a puzzling phenomenon in American religion. Respondents to religious polls in the United States typically self-select that at least ninety percent of them believe in God and eighty percent believe in Christ. But only sixty-five percent of Americans belong to a church, and it is common in established churches for half their reported membership to be inactive, many of whom are nonresident or cannot even be found. Why this precipitous decline that, in terms of actual participation, finds as many or more confessed believers outside the church as inside it? Insiders tend to blame the situation on the seductions of the world, which is doubtless the case in many instances. But increasingly I meet laypersons who have left the church only after careful consideration because they concluded that its ministers did not empower them to face the great issues of life with candor and courage. After exhausting their efforts to change the culture of the church without success, they felt that their only recourse was to find guidance outside their churches. Admittedly my evidence is only anecdotal, but in sixty years of ministry one does collect a lot of anecdotes!

At present, lay-clergy power struggles simmer beneath the surface in many congregations and denominations, but they are breaking into open warfare as seen in the rapid increase of involuntary terminations on the clergy side and church swapping on the laity side. Unless the "wall of hostility" between these two groups can be broken down, these disturbing trends are likely to accelerate. Such a breakthrough will begin only when we recover the consistent New Testament emphasis that Christ alone has gathered up all that is priestly in his finished work, hence his is the only ministry that we are called to perform. This means that priestly credentials come not from technical skills but from personal attachment to Christ, a relationship that is no respecter of ancestry, gender, or training. That dimly understood and seldom implemented doctrine of the "priesthood of all believers" means, at the very minimum, that every Christian is a minister and that this ministry is both spiritual and temporal, both vertical and horizontal, both in the church and in the world. There may well be legitimate distinctions in function based on varieties of gifts, but not on differences of status based on inherent privileges of rank. Both clergy and laity alike are to do the whole work of the church, which includes the offering of worship, the reaching of outsiders, the nurturing of disciples, the care of the flock, the delivering of the oppressed, and the overseeing of resources.

To some, this emphasis would seem to require that all formal church vocations be abolished and replaced by purely functional expressions of ministry. However, such an arrangement is not necessitated by the New Testament where at least embryonic ministerial roles began to emerge (Romans 12:6-8; 1 Cor. 12:8-10; Eph. 4:11). There, instead, we find in Eph. 4:11-12 an explicit rationale for clerical ministers that does not compromise but rather reinforces both the necessity and equality of lay ministers. This passage may be paraphrased: "God bestows particular gifts [that is, spiritual capacities and competencies] on certain persons to insure that essential functions will be discharged within the life of the church, but those so gifted are to fulfill these functions, not as an end in themselves, but rather with a view to the equipping of all God's people to do the work of the ministry so that the entire Body of Christ will be built up."[13]

In other words, those persons who specialize in ministry as a professional vocation by virtue of aptitude and training are to serve as *enablers* guiding all of the Christians who turn to them for help in becoming lay ministers. Far from exercising an exclusive ministry that cannot be shared, clerics are to be judged by the extent to which they are able to achieve a participatory partnership *in* ministry with those *to whom* they minister.

Sadly, many lay persons have been subordinated by the church for so long that they are just as reluctant to accept the full responsibilities of ministry as clergy are to share their calling with them. But only a full, not limited, partnership in priesthood involving all Christians will suffice to implement that astonishing New Testament transformation whereby an

---

[13]This paraphrase is based on a punctuation of the Greek text that corrects the "authorized" tradition of translation (KJV, RSV) along lines reflected in British translations (Phillips, NEB).

exclusive group existing for Israel was enlarged to include the entire new Israel that now existed for the whole world.

5

Beyond the Spiritual Barrier

I

We come, at last, to the final restriction built into the theological architecture of the Jerusalem Temple. It lay beyond the social barrier separating Gentile from Jew, the sexual barrier separating female from male, and the sacral barrier separating laity from clergy. Any worshiper able to penetrate this deeply into the holy precincts would enter the Court of Priests, a total area some 186 feet wide by 264 feet deep. Just as the Court of Priests was surrounded in U-shape fashion by the Court of Israel, so it surrounded in like manner the Sanctuary proper, which took up most of the available space.[1]

Moving due west from the upturned flagstones that defined the sacral barrier, one would soon pass around the massive altar (at least forty-eight feet square at its base), then mount a grand flight of twelve steps, interspersed with at least two landings, to reach the Temple Porch (Propylaeum). The façade of this vestibule was 150 feet high and 150 feet wide, with an open entrance sixty feet high and thirty feet wide (Josephus says 105 feet high and thirty-seven and one-

---

[1]Descriptions of the Sanctuary lying within the Court of Priests are found in Josephus, *Jewish War* 5.207-25; and in the Mishnah, *Middoth* 3.1--5:4.

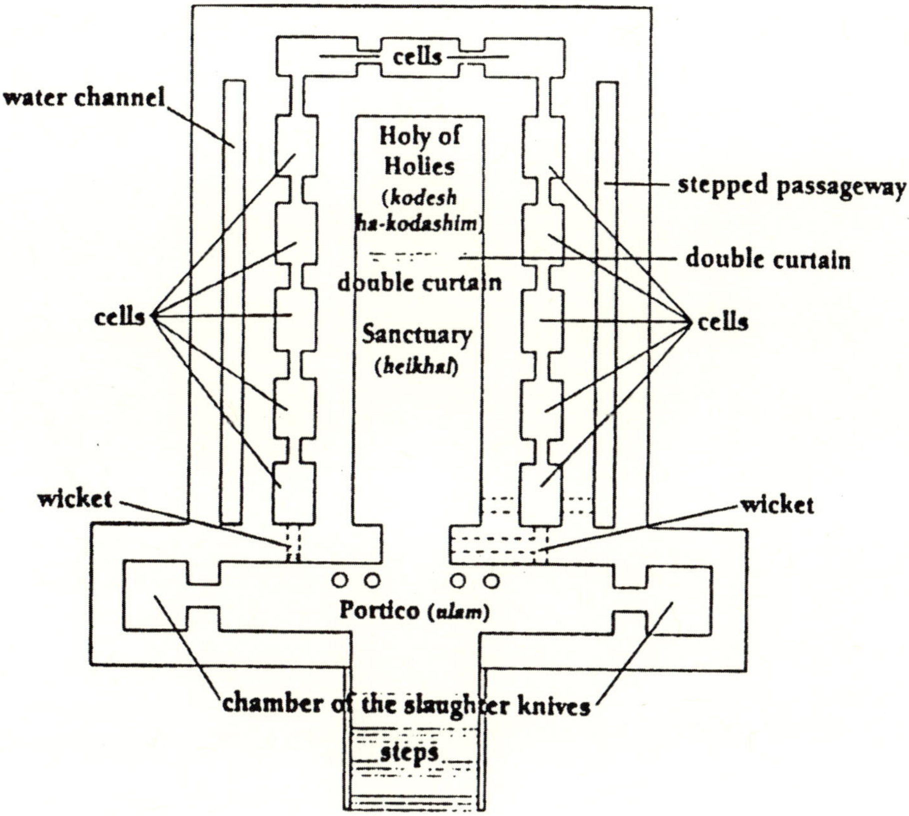

Plan of the Temple's Lower Story

half feet wide) enabling worshipers to see the front of the Temple proper, which was covered with gold.

Crossing the sixteen and one-half-foot-deep entrance hall, one then entered the Sanctuary itself through a double door thirty feet high and fifteen feet wide (Josephus says eighty-two and one-half feet high and twenty-four feet wide), over which hung a great golden vine. The main building was divided into two chambers: (1) The Holy Place (Hebrew *Hekal*), an area thirty feet wide and sixty feet deep containing the golden lampstand, the table of showbread, and the altar of incense. (2) The Holy of Holies (Hebrew *Debir*), also thirty feet wide but only thirty feet deep, which remained empty of furnishings because it was reserved exclusively as the dwelling place of God.

It was here that one reached the ultimate sanctity of the Temple. In the ten degrees of holiness defined by the Mishnah (*Kelim* 1.6-9), the Court of Israel was sixth, the Court of the Priests was seventh, the area from the Altar to the Porch was eighth, the Sanctuary was ninth, and the Holy of Holies within it was tenth. Only the priests on duty might enter the Holy Place to burn incense morning and afternoon, to trim the lampstand daily, and to supply the table with fresh showbread every Sabbath.[2] But the Holy of Holies was "unapproachable, inviolable, invisible to all" (Josephus, *Jewish*

---

[2]For details see the older work of Alfred Edersheim, *The Temple* (London: James Clarke, 1959) 152-94; and the more recent update of Emil Schürer, *The History of the Jewish People in the Age of Jesus Christ*, new English version rev. and ed. by Geza Vermes, Fergus Millar, and Matthew Black (Edinburgh: T. & T. Clark, 1979) 2:292-308. A partial reference to these arrangements is found in Luke 1:8-9.

War 5.219), "for none may enter therein save only the High Priest on the Day of Atonement" (Mishnah, *Kelim* 1.9).

Guarding this deepest secret was a double curtain, sixty feet high and thirty feet wide, that completely separated the Holy of Holies from the Holy Place (Mishnah, *Shekalim* 8.5). The outer curtain hung free on the south side (that is, it folded back to the right) while the inner curtain hung free on the north side (that is, it folded back to the left), with eighteen inches between them (Mishnah, *Yoma* 5.1; *Middoth* 4.7).

This meant that anyone seeking access to the Holy of Holies would have to part the outer veil at its left corner, walk the narrow eighteen-inch corridor between the two veils for its full length of thirty feet, then part the inner veil at its right corner. Both of these curtains, and the dividing space between them, were considered a single barrier in direct succession to the blue, purple, and red veil decorated with cherubim that hung both in the Mosaic Tabernacle (Ex. 26:31-35; Mishnah, *Yoma* 5.1) and in the Solomonic Temple (2 Chr. 3:14; Josephus, *Jewish Antiquities* 8.71-72).

Josephus also described a veil over the double door leading from the Temple Porch into the Holy Place: "of Babylonian tapestry, with embroidery of blue and fine linen, of scarlet also and purple, wrought with marvelous skills. Nor was this mixture of materials without its mystic meaning: it typified the universe" (*Jewish War* 5.212; cf. *Jewish Antiquities* 15.394-95). This hanging may have been the successor to the richly ornate screen covering the entrance to the tabernacle (Ex. 26:36; 36:37; cf. Philo, *Life of Moses* 2.101), which is referred to indirectly in Hebrews 9:3. By a fairly consistent use of different Hebrew and Greek words for the two Temple veils, it seems clear that this outer covering was not as significant as the inner curtain to which it led (cf. *Letter of Aristeas* 85-86; Mishnah, *Tamid* 7.1; Philo, *The Giants* 53).

Thus, we are left with the task of interpreting the last limitation of all—that innermost barrier of the Temple separating the human from the divine. At bottom, this arrangement was an attempt by Judaism to deal with the presence of God on earth.[3] The double veil served to symbolize that divine reality was supremely focused, and hence uniquely localized, in the Holy of Holies. This conviction, that God's earthly dwelling was concentrated at the heart of the Jerusalem Temple, had significant implications for the nature of Judaism. Only as we understand this claim will we be able to appreciate the New Testament affirmation that even this final divider was abolished by the work of Christ.

II

From the outset of its existence, Israel was profoundly aware of the presence of God in its midst, particularly in specific events, such as the Exodus, by which he revealed himself to his people and delivered them from their enemies. One of the earliest efforts to express this faith was the Mosaic tabernacle, a portable sanctuary to which God would descend, enveloping it with his glory (Ex. 33:9; 40:34-35; Num. 9:15-23).

---

[3]On the theme of the divine presence on earth, with special reference to the Temple, see W. J. Phythian-Adams, *The People and the Presence* (London: Oxford University Press, 1942); Yves M. J. Congar, *The Mystery of the Temple* (London: Burns & Oates, 1962); R. E. Clements, *God and Temple* (Philadelphia: Fortress, 1965). For a broader treatment of the presence of God as the basis of a biblical theology, see Samuel Terrien, *The Elusive Presence* (San Francisco: Harper and Row, 1979).

Although the tabernacle did tend to localize, centralize, and ritualize Israel's response to the divine presence, its very nature and function as a movable tent served as a constant reminder that Yahweh was not limited to any one location. He might temporarily "tabernacle" on earth to "meet" his people at specific times and places, but his primary dwelling was clearly in heaven.

This balanced tension between the universality and particularity of God's presence was modified by the establishment of one permanent shrine in Jerusalem under David and Solomon, as the martyr Stephen saw so clearly many centuries later (Acts 7:44-50). By the time of the Deuteronomic reform under Josiah (2 Kgs. 22:3--23:25), the Jerusalem Temple had become the exclusive worship center of the nation. Local sanctuaries were abolished and their priesthoods suppressed, causing personal religion to languish among the people. What we now call "civil religion" began to flourish in the capital city under the dominance of the king. The authorized priesthood became more professionalized, the ritual more formalized, leading to increasing veneration of the Temple as an end in itself. Eventually the Temple came to be seen as a unique guarantee of the presence and protection of God rather than as an institutional servant facilitating that sense in the lives of his people.

To be sure, these trends were met with blistering protests from the prophets of Israel (e.g. Amos 5:21-25; Isa. 1:11-17; Jer. 7:1-15), warnings that were confirmed by the events of the Exile which saw the vaunted Temple reduced to ruins. But if anything, the crisis of captivity only strengthened the determination to return to Jerusalem as the spatial center of the Jewish world and there to rebuild the Temple as tangible evidence of God's dwelling with his people. Even though

Ezekiel envisioned this restoration in idealized terms (Ezek. 40--48), he nevertheless retained and enlarged upon the Deuteronomic heritage by depicting a single, eternal sanctuary functioning as the centerpiece of a theocratic community (Ezek. 37:26-28). Historical reality proved much harsher than this dream, but prophets such as Haggai and Zechariah, and later leaders such as Ezra and Nehemiah, urged the nation to build back what they could as essential, not only to the fulfillment of their hopes, but to their very survival as the chosen people of God.

There is no need to recount the centuries leading up to the climax of this process in the Herodian Temple of New Testament times because the rationale was already firmly fixed in the aftermath of Exile. To summarize: all of Israel's existence was tempered by a tension between divine *presence* and human *place*. Holding these two realities together was the concept of a Promised Land as the locus of Israel's covenant with Yahweh.[4] Central to this theology was the certainty that God was with them, and that they were to be his chosen people, because he had given them a place on earth in which to dwell. This territorial imperative defined their peoplehood, enabling them to resist every threat of assimilation through conquest and dispersal. As long as they could cling to the land, or even to the hope of reclaiming it, they could endure as an entity in time and space. Without such rootage, they had no place in history.

---

[4]On the centrality of "the Land" for Judaism see W. D. Davies, *The Gospel and the Land: Early Christianity and Jewish Territorial Doctrine* (Berkeley: University of California Press, 1974); Walter Brueggeman, *The Land* (Philadelphia: Fortress Press, 1977).

Thus did the givenness of the Holy Land rally the Jewish people wherever they might be scattered. But even a place as small as Palestine needed a unifying hub, which need was met by the capital city, Jerusalem. Nor could the localizing tendency stop there. If the Holy City was the center of the Holy Land, then the Holy Mount was the center of the Holy City, and the Holy Place was the center of the Holy Mount, and the Holy of Holies was the center of the Holy Place! This jealously guarded spot was the ultimate bastion of Israel's claim to *a place on earth with God*. That is why, in the great war with Rome of AD 70, the defenders of the nation retreated first to Jerusalem, then to Mount Zion, then to the Sanctuary itself in the conviction that if they lost this last bit of sacred soil they would perish as the hereditary-national-cultural religion which they were meant to be.[5]

To be sure, Judaism was fully aware of the universality of God; indeed, such a premise was inherent in the monotheism which it championed. But Judaism did not hold that the presence on earth of this universal God somehow dissolved the particularities of human society or collapsed the continuities of human history. On the contrary, God's covenant love was seen precisely in his condescension to choose a specific race ("the seed of Abraham") at a specific place ("the land which I gave unto your fathers") with a specific nation ("the throne of David") as the instrument of his purpose for the world. That was the essence of the secret

---

[5]For details see S. G. F. Brandon, *The Fall of Jerusalem and the Christian Church* (London: S.P.C.K., 1957) 154-77; W. R. Farmer, *Maccabees, Zealots, and Josephus* (New York: Columbia University Press, 1956), 84-124; Martin Goodman, *Rome and Jerusalem: The Clash of Ancient Civilizations* (New York: Alfred A. Knopf, 2007).

guarded by the veil: *universality dwelling in particularity* (that is, the God of all lands in *one* land, the God of all peoples with *one* people, the God of all nations with *one* nation). If that premise should be undermined, then Judaism as it then existed would be seriously compromised.

III

As the infancy narratives of the Gospels make clear, Jesus was born and bred in the bosom of this Jewish particularity (Mt. 1–2; Lk. 1–2). The opening chapters of Luke especially reflect the rootage of his ministry in the Temple, synagogue, and piety of the land. The hymns of annunciation, for example, are filled with traditional expectations of a messiah who would restore the throne of David, save the people from their enemies, and reign over the kingdom of the house of Jacob forever (Lk. 1:32-35, 54-55, 68-75). The sacred story begins in the Holy Place itself (Lk. 1:5-23), just as it ends in the Temple (Lk. 24:53), leading one to suppose that Jesus would have supported the theology of the veil which defined the presence of God in terms of its focus behind the innermost barrier.

But no sooner did his ministry begin than Jesus challenged this whole understanding of the relation between divine presence and earthly place. In his wilderness temptation he rejected the messianic notions of a miraculous appearing at the Temple (Mal. 3:1) or of subduing worldly kingdoms such as Rome (Mt. 4:5-10). Instead, he launched his mission in obscure Galilee, of all places, and dared to assert that the long-awaited kingdom of God was "at hand" *there* rather than in Jerusalem (Mt. 4:12-17). The very name "Galilee," which was an abbreviation of the Hebrew phrase, "Circle of the Gentiles" (*Galil-ha-goyim*), signified the pagan periphery of the Holy Land (Isa. 9:1). To say that God was ready to begin his earthly reign as king in this despised "land of darkness," rather than in the capital city of Jerusalem, contradicted the prevailing Jewish notion that the New Age would begin at, and converge on, the Temple in the Holy City.

As Jesus' ministry progressed, the "secret of the kingdom" (Mk. 4:11)—that is, the mystery of how it could be inaugurated under such obscure circumstances—was made increasingly clear. For wherever Jesus cast out demons, the reign of God arrived in that particular life (Mt. 12:28; Luke 11:20). Wherever he told parables, the reality of the transcendent realm was made visible for those with eyes to see (Mt. 13:10-17). In other words, the kingdom had suddenly drawn "near" because *he* was near. It could be "entered" in Galilee because *he* was in Galilee. This implied that the climactic expression of God's presence on earth, which the Jews and Jesus alike described as the effective establishment of his eternal kingship, was now linked, not to a fixed *place* in Jerusalem, but to a mobile *person* on ministry.

That being the case, it is not surprising to find a few instances when God's dwelling in the life of Jesus was likened to the Divine dwelling in the Temple. On one such occasion, Jesus defended his disciples against the charge of unlawfully eating on the Sabbath by pointing out that David once "entered the house of God and ate the bread of the Presence," which was lawful only for priests (Mt. 12:1-5). By adding, "I tell you, *something greater than the temple is here*" (v. 6), he implied that his disciples had every prerogative of the priesthood because they served a greater Temple than the one in Jerusalem. Since Jewish theology viewed that latter Temple as unique, to say that another and greater Temple was located elsewhere (*"here"*) called into question the very rationale on which the Jerusalem Temple was based. There could be no reason to define and protect the presence of God with a veil if, in fact, that presence was more manifest in the ministry of Jesus than in the Holy of Holies. Such may have been the experience of an inner group of disciples on the Mount of Transfiguration (Mt. 17:1-8; Mk. 9:2-8; Lk. 9:28-36). In his impetuous response to the glorification of the master, Peter failed to see that "there was no need for three tabernacles, nor even for one. For Jesus was Himself the new tabernacle of the Divine glory, who gathered up in his own person all the transient and fragmentary revelations of the past." [6]

In one saying with revolutionary implications, Jesus indicated his intention to transform the Temple as it then existed in Judaism (Mt. 26:61; Mk. 14:58; Mt. 27:39-40; Mk. 15:29-30; Jn. 2:19; cf. Acts 6:13-14). Although the exact wording in the fivefold attestation of this pronouncement varies, all accounts have three elements in common whose meaning is clear from related passages:

> (1) Jesus clearly predicted the destruction of the Jerusalem Temple right down to its innermost sanctuary (*naos*). The Jewish leadership would inflict this catastrophe upon themselves in the near future because of their false reliance on the Temple as an inviolable bulwark against other nations instead of making the Temple a worldwide center for the evangelization of the Gentiles (Lk. 19:41-44; Mt. 23:37-39; Lk. 13:34-35; Mt. 24:1-2; Mk. 13:1-2; Lk. 21:5-

---

[6] G. B. Caird, "The Transfiguration," *The Expository Times* 67 (July 1956): 293.

> 6). His disciples, therefore, could simply dispense with the Temple as with a withered tree; for them, the whole Mount of the Lord might as well be dumped into the Dead Sea (Mt. 21:21)!
>
> (2) Jesus just as confidently anticipated that he would raise up in spiritual form ("not made with hands") that sacred shrine (*naos*) now marked for destruction in its physical form.
>
> (3) Furthermore, mention that this replacement would transpire in the space of "three days" meant that it would be accomplished by his death and resurrection, which would occur during the same interval of time (Mk. 8:31; 9:31; 10:34, and parallels).

In short, Jesus believed that when he died, the old Temple would die with him; but when he arose, a new Temple would rise with him. The latter stage launched by the resurrection, that of building the church as a new Temple, will be considered in the next chapter. For now, let us concentrate on the earlier developments launched by his death, that of breaking down the last barrier that remained in the Jewish Temple.

All of the Synoptic Gospels record that at the very moment when Jesus breathed his last, "the curtain of the Temple was torn in two from top to bottom" (Mt. 27:50-51; Mk. 15:37-38; Lk. 23:45-46). No symbolism could have been more dramatic—or should we say traumatic?—for this event was viewed, not as an angry reprisal against the Jews by followers of Jesus, but as a solemn act of judgment by God himself.

Human hands could never reach up and rend that sixty-foot veil "*from top to bottom*." Instead, God reached down and ripped it open, thereby exposing its deepest secret as barren, bereft of the presence it was constructed to contain. In that awful moment of midday darkness, God himself violated the ultimate mystery of the Temple by declaring that he was uniquely present, not on a hill of splendor in the Holy of Holies with its multiple barriers, but on a hill of shame in the vulnerable nakedness of his only Son.

But this act of judgment, by which the divine glory fled from hiding behind a curtain to be exposed upon a cross, was also viewed in early Christianity as an act of mercy by which totally new access was provided into the very presence of God. Jesus, their "high priest," had "gone as a forerunner on [their] behalf . . . into the inner shrine behind the curtain," but with this decisive difference from Judaism: he had invited all of his followers to join him there (Heb. 6:19-20)! The mood in which that new venture was undertaken is beautifully described farther on in Hebrews: "Therefore, my friends, since we have *confidence* to enter the *sanctuary* by the blood [that is, death] of Jesus, by the *new and living way* that he opened for us *through the curtain,* (that is, through his flesh, and since we have a great priest over the house of God, let us *approach* with a true heart in *full assurance* of faith" (10:19-22; author's italics).

What an incredible contrast! In Judaism, only the high priest, one male of selective ancestry and unique position, was entitled to penetrate the veil only once a year, on the Day of Atonement. The Mishnah records that even when it was necessary to make repairs to the walls of the Holy of Holies, workmen would approach the chamber through an upper story or overhead attic where there were openings through which they could be let down in boxes. This was done so that their feet would not touch the floor and their eyes would not feast upon the room (*Middoth* 4.5). In Christianity, on the other hand, ordinary believers were urged to "keep on coming" to God beyond the curtain, regardless of their ancestry, gender, or nationality. These two different approaches reflect nothing less than a revolution in the sense of access to the presence of God on earth.

What exactly had happened to the Jewish doctrine of God's presence in a particular place as symbolized by the veil guarding the Holy of Holies? The Gospel of John describes the Christian transformation most profoundly. In the John's prologue (Jn. 1:1-18) it interprets the incarnation as the presence ("Word") of God "lived" on earth in "flesh," that is, in the historical life of Jesus Christ (Jn. 1:14). As of old, God "pitched a tent" on earth, but this time it was not in a specific place but in a specific person, so that all who received him by faith might "behold" the long-concealed "glory" of the Father. Now the divine presence was so uniquely focused in Jesus that he became a living "Holy of Holies" with his "flesh" serving as the curtain that enclosed the Shekinah glory (Heb. 10:20b). Because the locus of God's presence was now personalized rather than institutionalized, that meant it was now movable and thus no longer tied to any one holy mountain (Jn. 4:20-24). The concept of "place" was retained in that God was still uniquely present at a defined spot on earth—that is, wherever Jesus was!—but this new understanding separated the sense of "place" from any particular land or nation or people and focused instead on God's mobility (Acts 7:44-50).

Because of this interpretation of what incarnation meant for the theology of the Temple, the Fourth Evangelist was able to append a most incisive comment to his recording of the New Temple pronouncement (Jn. 2:19). The Jewish retort that Jesus could hardly build a Temple in three days, when they had already been at the same task for forty-six years, led the Evangelist to explain, "But he was speaking of *the temple of his body*" (Jn. 2:21).

This interpretation had two crucial applications. Initially, it meant that the earthly body of Jesus could be viewed as a new Temple because God was uniquely present in his flesh-and-blood historical existence. Subsequently, it meant that, after the resurrection of Jesus, his followers collectively became his body on earth, and their historical existence as the church could also be viewed as a new Temple because God was still uniquely present in their corporate life through the Spirit of Christ. There we reach the last step in the universalizing of the sense of "place" which began with the incarnation. God's presence was still defined in terms of a specific locale, that is, wherever the "body of Christ" was concretely manifested, but such communities were now scattered all over the earth. One centralized holy *place* had been superseded by a decentralized holy *people!*

What we have here, in essence, is the shift from a *centripetal* theology of the Temple, which sought to centralize the experience of God around a single holy place in Jerusalem, to a *centrifugal* theology of the Temple, which sought to decentralize the experience of God by scattering living sanctuaries wherever the gospel might spread. That shift, as the martyr Stephen saw so clearly, did not contradict Old Testament theology but rather restored its original balance between the universality and the particularity of God's presence on earth. The apostle Paul realized that this centrifugal thrust was essential to a worldwide missionary enterprise. That is why he regularly reminded Gentile congregations in such pagan cities as Corinth that they actually *were* the "temple" of God (e.g., 1 Cor. 3:16-17; 2 Cor. 6:16). The Greek word that Paul invariably used for "temple" (*naos*) referred, not to the outer precincts (*hieron*) provided for Gentiles, but to the inner Sanctuary itself, which was a way of saying that the Holy of Holies of God's dwelling lay at the heart of their common life together.

IV

We now ask what this audacious claim, that even the final barrier into the presence of God has been broken down, means for our spiritual life today? As the context of our key verse in Ephesians 2:14 makes clear, the new situation occasioned by this development is one where all believers alike now have equal "*access* in one Spirit to the Father" (v. 18). What are the implications of affirming that, through Christ, God is available to every person regardless of ethnic origin, gender, or vocation?

Consider first the consequences of this claim for the false dichotomy which some Christians try to maintain between personal evangelism and social justice. The mood of the times as this book is being written is one of so-called "conservatism" which, under the banner of that once-noble word, would turn its back on the battle for human dignity and equality that obviously has not yet been won. On every hand one hears that churches and their leaders should concentrate exclusively on "soul-winning" and avoid such "controversial" issues as racial discrimination, the rights of women, or the reform of clerical authoritarianism. But the sequence of our Temple symbolism provides a needed corrective to this one-sided perspective. For one could not even consider the question of entering the presence of God in the Jerusalem

Temple until the social and sexual and sacral walls had been surmounted. An overriding passion of Paul's life was to let Christ break down every system of subordination and exclusiveness based on inherited human differences so that *everyone together* could then move into the presence of God.

Still today there are prominent religious leaders who, in theory, seem committed to worldwide evangelism but who, in practice, show an interest only in reaching that white, middle-class segment of society that will support their religious empires. Ironically, some of those who shout most loudly that the barrier between God and every person has been abolished, still maintain social structures that make people feel superior or inferior in relation to one another. Paul knew that "barriers of hostility" between people create barriers to God and, likewise, that access to one another in love is an integral part of experiencing access to God. That is why he combined into a single phrase the two facets that we often keep separate by describing Christ's work on the cross as reconciling us all "*to God in one body*," thereby bringing our hostility, whether toward God or toward others, to an end (Eph. 2:16).

The Jerusalem Temple was both the locus of God's presence on earth and a human response to that presence. Likewise our churches, each as a "temple of God," offer, not only an encounter with God, but also an encounter with those who have met God. What Paul saw so clearly was that these human and divine aspects of the Temple must be consistent. If our relationship to God has been transformed, then our relation to others is to be transformed as well. If a holy God dwelling in utter perfection is willing to remove every restriction and receive sinful humanity, how much more should we be willing to set aside such arbitrary distinctions as race, sex, or status and just as freely receive one another!

A second implication of breaking down that final barrier is that each individual is offered a direct encounter with God. The Holy of Holies was empty of human furnishings because, when one reached God himself, such paraphernalia was unnecessary. Once the high priest entered beyond the veil, he left behind the pageantry of worship, the elaborate sacrifices, the music of the Levites, the gathered people, and the symbolism of the buildings. Just so, finally we are to move beyond the minister who guides us, the hymns that uplift us, the architecture designed to impress us, in order to deal directly with God and his people in a spirit of openness. For the collapse of that innermost curtain means that we have a God who does not "keep his distance" but can be reached by the venture of faith open to all.

Actually, it may be disconcerting for nominal Christians to discover that they are now expected to negotiate that final passage into the very presence of God which long ago was entrusted only to the high priest. We saw in the previous chapter than an unfortunate proxy relationship was introduced into Temple worship when laypersons were required to hand over their sacrifices to an authorized priesthood who then stood between them and God. Now we must push this question of mediation to its final resolution, for the unveiled Holy of Holies means, to borrow from an old gospel song, that there is "*nothing* between my soul and the Savior."[7] On the journey to God there are a host of helps, both personal and procedural. But that journey ends at the veil,

---

[7]Charles A. Tindley, "Nothing Between," stanza 1.

where even our finest worship aids can do no more. Beyond the veil there is nothing to bring but ourselves, for there is nothing left to do but deal with God on a person-to-person basis.

How slow we are to admit that many have never walked through the final curtain that Christ died to tear open (Mk. 15:37-39). A great host of sincere Christians, like their Jewish forebears, have never moved beyond a mediated religious experience to an unmediated encounter with God. They worship in buildings that somebody else built, sing hymns that somebody else composed, pray prayers that somebody else voices, listen to sermons that somebody else preaches, give money that somebody else spends, confess creeds that somebody else wrote. And all of this is fine—unless it goes no farther! For these and other religious practices are designed to bring us to the final barrier, to the edge of the mystery, to the door of the secret place of the Most High. But if we stop before that veil, then our religion is only secondhand, nourished not by God himself but by experiences that others have had with God.

The church is a living repository of human responses to the presence of God. That is how our great traditions have developed. Somebody penetrated the veil and came back to tell others about it. But that testimony *about* God, even when it is found in Holy Scripture, is no substitute for a firsthand experience *with* God. And what Christianity dares to assert is that such an encounter is not reserved for a few saints and mystics but is open to the humblest believers who have Christ as their guide. The Christian life finally becomes parasitic when it consists only of eating fruit nourished by another's root. It is when we sink our own roots into the reality of God that we discover what lies beyond the ultimate barrier in the Holy of Holies.

A third consequence of the conviction that God is not remote but accessible lies in the new relationship of holiness to worldliness. The Jerusalem Temple was deliberately designed to guard the Shekinah glory from impious eyes. All of the multiple barriers which we have analyzed served as buffers between the sacred and the secular. The ten grades of holiness to which we have repeatedly referred simply applied a theology of purity to this architectural symbolism. But when Christianity redefined each Christian community scattered about the Greco-Roman Empire as a living sanctuary (1 Pet. 2:5), suddenly God was relocated, if we may so express it. Now his presence was no longer pinpointed in the innermost recesses of an elaborate stonework that literally could and did serve as a fortress; instead, the divine presence was thrust out into the arena of everyday life. For centuries, the supreme symbol of God's presence had been a perfect thirty-foot cube covered with gold (2 Chron. 3:8-9), whereas now that august symbolism was being transferred to a body of Christians including those who had formerly been immoral, idolaters, adulterers, homosexuals, thieves, the greedy, drunkards, revilers, and robbers (1 Cor. 6:9-11, 19).

What a comedown for God to move from his world-famous Temple in Jerusalem to an exasperatingly immature company of Christians in Corinth! But if he gave up quarters better suited to his majesty, he found quarters better suited to his mercy. For now nobody was really an outsider any longer, looking up at that summit on Mount Zion which few could attain. Instead, since the Shekinah glory had, so to speak, shifted from the penthouse to the basement, it now lay at the raw, sore heart of things, waiting to be discovered by anyone willing to be drawn into the life of those ordinary Christians in Corinth or Ephesus or Rome. Already the incarnation was a scandal because it meant that "the fullness of God" had dwelt in the life of an obscure carpenter from Nazareth (Col. 1:19). But now his followers became, if anything, an even greater scandal because Christ *in them* was believed to be "the hope of *glory*" (Col. 1:27).

One of the most cherished expectations in Judaism was that the glory of the Lord would one day shine forth from the Temple on Mount Zion.[8] To insist instead that such hope was misplaced, and that God's great redemption could best be seen not in the old Temple which the Jews had finally finished building in Jerusalem but in the New Temple which was still being built as the Body of Christ, is a claim that forever defines the essential difference between Christianity and Judaism.

In three summary statements, Thomas W. Gillespie has well expressed the significance and relevance of the insights clarified in this chapter:

> The New Testament reinterpretation of the temple concept has profound consequences for our understanding of the popular distinction between sacred and secular spheres of life. God's temple-presence as a people-presence means that the profane (from the Latin *profanus*, meaning "before the temple") recedes before the advance of the community in its ministry to the world. Because

---

[8]The conception is rather complex. For a helpful summary of the evidence see Joachim Jeremias, *Jesus' Promise to the Nations* (London: SCM Press, 1958) 56-70.

> God is where the people are, corporately or individually, wherever they are becomes a sacred place.

A more radical reinterpretation of the traditional temple concept is difficult to imagine. God's "dwelling" upon earth is a people rather than a building, a holy people "set apart" for God rather than coddled in seclusion, a people called by God to the living of salvation in the matrix of everyday life rather than delivered from life's care and responsibilities, a people who live "before God" at all times and in all places rather than lead double lives in segregated sacred and secular compartments. Ministry in such a temple-community can only be worldward in its thrust.

God's temple-people go forth into the world under orders, recognizing no artificial distinctions between sacred and secular spheres of sovereignty, living salvation in the place of their individual calling, invading the precincts of the profane under the banner of God's claim upon all the earth. God's "royal priesthood" serves in the world beneath the high priesthood of Christ, enjoying direct access to the divine presence, using that access to intercede for the world with which it has identified itself in obedience to the model of the earthly ministry of Jesus. In grateful response to the atoning death of Christ, the people of God's own possession offer their individual lives in all of their actuality as living sacrifices, and express his life commitment in the daily sacrifices of word and deed which are "pleasing" to God because they bear witness to his love and purpose for the world.[9]

[9]Thomas W. Gillespie, "The Laity in Biblical Perspective," *Theology Today* 36 (October 1979): 320, 322, 327.

6

The Wall Builder

I

Up to this point, our tour of the Temple precincts has concentrated on the demolition work of the New Joshua, before whose assault the multiple walls separating worshipers from each other and from God came tumbling down. Standing now at the innermost heart of the Holy Place, we see that the gospel of Jesus Christ levels every barrier that would deny any person a direct encounter with the Divine.

But if we were to stop here, amid the ruins which the Great Abolitionist inflicted on his ancestral religion, it could leave the impression that Christ was a rebel concerned only to shatter inherited customs and conventions, leaving in their place an idealized worship, completely divorced from the social realities of historical existence. Even though the fellowship of heaven will transcend differences of ancestry and nationality and gender and vocational status, these distinctions crucially affect our lives here on earth. Then must all of this wall-breaking which we have traced be viewed finally as an effort to escape prematurely into an other-worldliness that is blind to the constraints of human nature?

Nothing could be farther from the truth, as is clear from the context of our primary passage. Ephesians 2:11-22 is

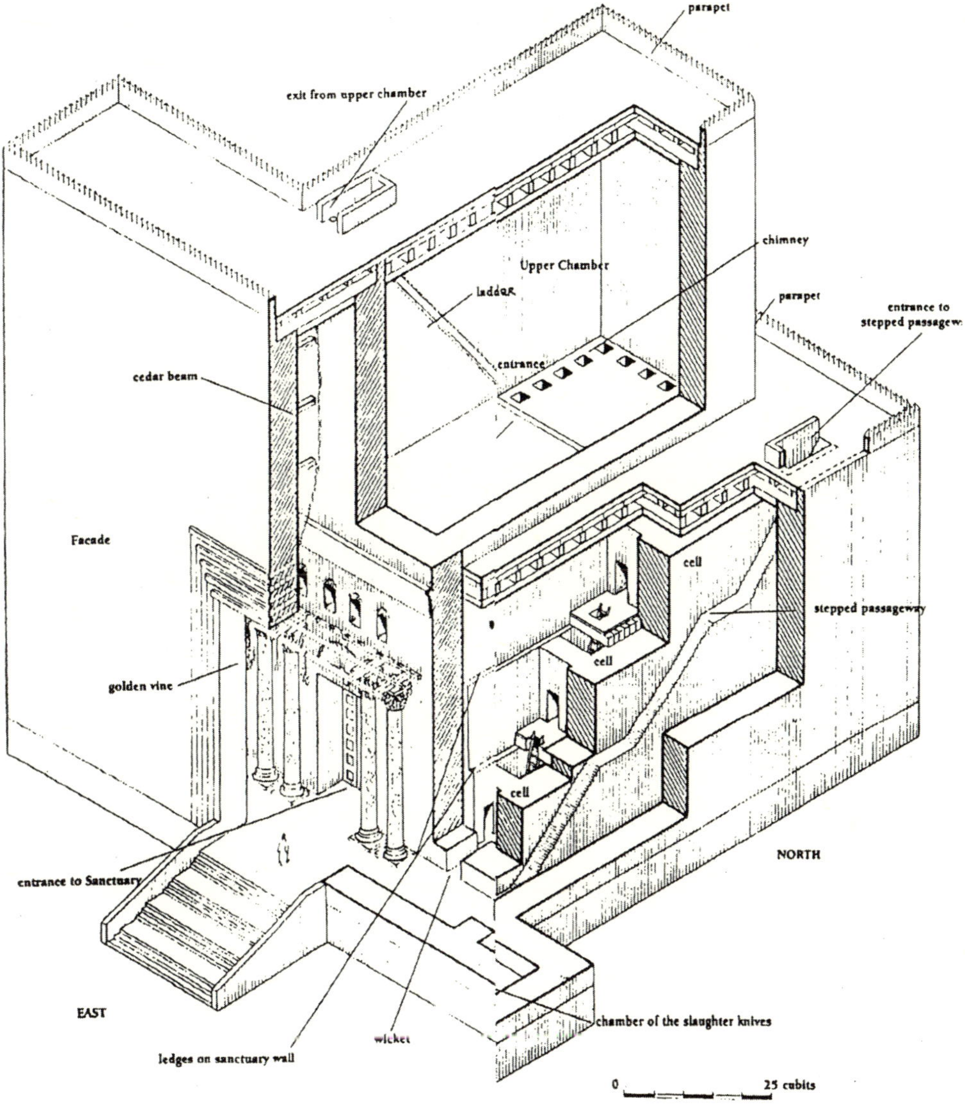
parapet
exit from upper chamber
chimney
Upper Chamber
ladder
parapet
entrance to
stepped passagew
entrance
cedar beam
Facade
cell
stepped passageway
cell
golden vine
cell
NORTH
entrance to Sanctuary
EAST
chamber of the slaughter knives
wicket
ledges on sanctuary wall
0
25 cubits

The Temple

carefully balanced to portray both the destructive and the constructive work of Jesus Christ. First, the negative work of demolition is described in verses 14-18: He has "broken down" the dividing wall of hostility (v. 14), "abolished" the law understood as a social code (v. 15), and "killed" (put to death) all human hatred by means of his cross (v. 16). Then the positive work of edification is described in verses 19-22: We are "built" upon the foundation which has Christ Jesus as its cornerstone (v. 20), "joined [fit] together" into a holy sanctuary (v. 21), and "built together spiritually" for a dwelling place of God in the Spirit (v. 22).

By the repeated application of masonry metaphors to Christians at the climax of this passage, Paul emphasized that Christ was not against walls as such. On the contrary, he battered down one kind of wall in order to put a better kind of wall in its place. Jesus was the implacable foe of every kind of wall that divided mankind into hostile camps, thereby raising barriers to oneness with each other and with God. But he was the architect of walls that united believers in peace and provided them equal access to the Father "in one Spirit" (v. 18). To understand better his positive role in relation to walls, we now sketch the background of the wall-*building* image from the Old Testament, the ministry of Jesus, and the other writings of Paul.[1]

---

[1]An intriguing meditation on this evidence by Jonathan Graham, *The Office of a Wall* (London: Faith Press, 1966) has influenced the section that follows.

II

The biblical story of redemption begins outside a walled garden where mankind was banished from the presence of God (Gen. 3:24). It ends with the redeemed inside a walled city whose boundaries are defined by the presence of the Lord God Almighty and the Lamb (Rev. 21:15-27). In between these outer limits lies the long search for a way that leads from exclusion to inclusion, with a gate that admits those separated from God to acceptance by God.

Israel arrived at its Promised Land as a fledgling nation of nomads accustomed to a migratory life in tents amid the open desert spaces. So intimidated were they by the walled cities of the Canaanites that they developed a "grasshopper complex" in the face of these fixed fortifications (Num. 13:17-33). But eventually, under leaders such as Joshua and David, they learned to subdue not only the oasis city of Jericho (Joshua 6:1-21) but the mountain stronghold of Jerusalem (2 Sam. 5:6-10). Quickly adjusting to urban life, they copied the pattern of their pagan predecessors by strengthening the walls of the Holy City as well as the Temple that came to be centralized there (1 Kgs. 3:1).

Three factors, however, required Israel to understand these walls differently from the way that the Canaanites understood their fortifications (Deut. 1:28). First, the prophets constantly reminded Zion that there was no security in trusting earthly battlements, however massive. Walls on the outside were worthless against pride, arrogance, or corruption on the inside (Isa. 1:2-8; 5:5-7; Mic. 3:9-12; Jer. 11:9-17). Secondly, the psalmists redefined the whole purpose of Jerusalem's walls in terms of their function to designate the dwelling place of God rather than in terms of their traditional function as military fortifications to repulse the enemy (Psa. 46:4-5; 48:1-3, 12-14; 84:1-4; 87:1-2; 100:4). Finally, because of this religious definition, earthly walls were seen to be completely inadequate to contain the universal presence of God (Isa. 66:1-4). All of these factors, acting together, set the stage for what we may call the spiritualization of the concept of divine walls.

The climax of this development for the Old Testament came during the postexilic period when Judaism had to decide how to claim the promise that God would rebuild the broken walls of Jerusalem (Isa. 44:26-28; 45:13; 49:14-18; 54:11-14). Nehemiah chose to erect a physical wall that would separate the Holy City from everything foreign (Neh. 2:1-20; 6:15-16; 12:27-30; 13:23-31). But Zechariah opted for a vision of Jerusalem "inhabited as villages *without walls* . . . For I will be to her *a wall of fire* all around it, says the Lord, and I will be the glory within it" (Zech. 2:4-5). In place of the stone walls that had afforded little protection against the Babylonians (Lam. 1:10; 2:7-9), the alternative was to seek security in the spiritual bulwark of God's salvation (Isa. 26:1; 60:18).

Jesus shared the prophetic foreboding that not even the most impressive stones could protect Jerusalem and its Temple from an enemy if the people were not obedient to the will of God (Lk. 19:41-44; Mt. 23:37-39; Mk. 13:1-2). But he also embraced the prophetic conviction that the loss of physical walls could be the prelude to the discovery of spiritual walls that God's redemption could provide, not walls of stone but walls of fire! This twofold understanding was expressed most clearly in the New Temple saying which was partially analyzed in the preceding chapter. The Jews, with their misplaced confidence in tangible walls, would see their precious Temple and Holy City reduced to ruins, but in "three days"—the "little while" of God's redemption through the death and resurrection of Jesus—a Temple building "not made with hands" would take its place (Mt. 26:61; 27:39-40; Mk. 14:58; 15:29-30, Jn. 2:19).

It is remarkable that all five records of this pronouncement clearly balance the ruin of the existing Temple with its rebuilding as a spiritual Temple. Even the enemies of Jesus, acting as false witnesses at his trial, were forced to concede that his ultimate intention was not destructive but constructive. The insistence that Jesus would raise up the very sanctuary which was to be demolished, though in spiritual rather than in physical form, proves that he was not against walls as such but only against those walls made "by hand" rather than by God (Acts 7:48; 17:24; Heb. 9:11, 24). Just as Jesus would be resurrected as the same person, though in spiritual form, so the Temple would be resurrected as the same sanctuary, though in spiritual form (Jn. 2:21).

Based directly on this premise, Paul could without hesitation refer to Christian churches, such as the struggling Gentile congregation at Corinth, as *the temple* of God (1 Cor. 3:16-17; 6:19; 2 Cor. 6:16). Always Paul used the word for the Sanctuary itself (*naos*) to refer to Christians who had no buildings. Never did he use it for the Holy Place in Jerusalem. Conversely, Paul never used the word for the outer Temple precincts with its system of walls (*hieron*) to refer to Christians. His only use of that word referred to priestly arrangements in Jerusalem. This pattern of usage led him to develop in Ephesians 2:20-22 the climactic expression of the New Temple concept, where a series of masonry metaphors traces each step in the building process.

First, the Apostle pictured a living "foundation" of apostles and prophets, at the beginning edge of which God, the master builder, placed Christ as the chief cornerstone determining the lie of the whole construction.[2] Every person who builds life on the rock that is Christ (1 Peter 2:4-5) comprises the leading wall of this holy sanctuary (Ephesians 2:20). Unlike the Jerusalem Temple built of stone, which may have been finished about the time Ephesians was written, this new temple built of lives transformed by Christ is never finished but continues to "grow" piece by piece as converts are added to the church through its missionary activity (v. 21). The most emphatic point Paul wished to make in this regard was that even outsiders, the "strangers and sojourners" of v. 19, are being incorporated into this living structure which now houses the dwelling place of God on earth (v. 22).

Anyone familiar with the incredibly impressive stone-work of the Jerusalem Temple (Mk. 13:1) could not help being struck by the forcefulness of this comparison. For the construction of the Christian edifice depended for its stability, not on the extreme care with which each stone was sized and dressed to fit perfectly into the overall design. An ancient tradition has it that when the first Temple was built by Solomon, "it was with stone prepared at the quarry so that neither hammer nor axe nor any tool of iron was heard in the temple, while it was being built" (1 Kings 6:7). Just so, Paul here pictured a collection of lives that formerly had nothing in common first being shaped through union with Christ into the likeness of his image; then being mortised together with

---

[2]The choice of "cornerstone" rather than "keystone" for the imagery of Jesus Christ in Ephesians 2:20 follows R. J. McKelvey, "Christ the Cornerstone," *New Testament Studies* 8 (1962): 352-59; *The New Temple* (London: Oxford University Press, 1969) 195-204.

each other as tightly as the Temple stones in Jerusalem that have endured to this day! It would be hard to think of a more powerful picture than that of a growing Temple wall to express the interlocking of disparate lives at the most intimate level imaginable.

With this stunning imagery clarified, we are now ready to contrast the walls that Christ died to break down with the ones that he lives to build up. The old walls were physical, "made with hands"; the new walls are spiritual, "not made with hands." The old walls were constructed of stone, therefore inert and immovable; the new walls are constructed of people, therefore living and growing. The old walls were barriers, separating hostile enemies; the new walls are unifiers, encouraging loving relationships. Most important, the old walls were guardians of the Holy of Holies designed to keep everyone at a distance from the presence of God; the new walls are themselves the Holy of Holies, designed to facilitate an encounter with God's presence for every person regardless of human qualifications. These distinctions prepare us to grasp the central truth in the biblical theology of walls: *Christ demolished every unworthy wall that generated hostility so that, in their place, God could fashion his people into true walls that enshrine his presence here on earth!*[3]

---

[3]I have omitted from this swift sketch any reference to the walled heavenly city in Ezekiel 48:30-35 and in Revelation 21:15-27. In both cases the identity of the city is defined by the divine presence ("The Lord is there"), and in both cases the walls have twelve gates the better to admit all who are worthy. It seems to me that this imagery, while very impressive, nevertheless lacks the profundity of the Pauline solution to the problem of walls. For the apocalyptic seers, walls remain as separate barriers standing between insiders and outsiders, whereas for the Apostle *we become the walls themselves* and so lose the freedom to construct any external structure as the

III

Utilizing this Pauline insight, that we are not to build walls that divide but to become walls that unite, let us now explore more deeply our role as "living stones" in that spiritual house which is Christ's Body, the church (1 Pet. 2:5). Walls have three essential functions that we are called upon to fulfill in the New Temple of God.

(1) *To define.* Walls organize space. They announce where something *is* located. In a home they mark off where to eat and sleep and work and play. On a campus they identify where the various branches of knowledge are taught. Fences on a farm say that one parcel of land is to be plowed and another is for grazing. By taming the limitlessness of space, they organize an impossible pluralism of opportunities into manageable units for which different persons may accept responsibility. There can be no meaningful stewardship without boundaries that limit the duties and privileges of finite persons. In a word, walls "contain," and therefore make tolerable, the endless complexity of life.

Because walls combat chaos and confusion, they are needed in the spiritual realm as well. In his poem, "City without Walls," W. H. Auden depicts the desolation that comes from being captive to "the Unbounded," from living

---

symbol of our superiority over others. As in Ezekiel and Revelation, the walls in Ephesians 2:19-22 have been *spiritualized* and so removed from the centuries of hostility that accumulated around tangible barriers. But Paul seems to have gone beyond this in that his walls have also been *personalized* to function as instruments of unification here and now on earth instead of as instruments of separation one day in heaven.

life in "unpolicied spaces."[4] The timid, tolerant mood of our times encourages us to draw no lines, to take no stands, to reject no options, to remain perpetually open to whatever may come along. But if the house of faith has no walls, then, finally, we can never find our own family in terms of those who have chosen to "enter" the kingdom of God (Mk. 10:23-24). Every wanderer in "unpolicied spaces" should never forget that to be "*in* Christ" is to be *somewhere* specific.

Dietrich Bonhoeffer was driven by the demonic alternatives lurking all about him to stress God's need for a clearly defined place where his truth would be visible in the life of committed followers. "The Body of Christ takes up physical space here on earth. By becoming human Christ claims a place among us human beings... the incarnation does entail the claim for space granted on earth, and anything that takes up space is visible. Thus the body of Jesus Christ can only be a visible Body, or else it is not a Body at all."[5] That is why we must now speak of the living-space (*Lebensraum*) of the visible church community."[6] In order to secure such space, the Church remains "in the world in order to engage the world in a frontal assault"[7] and claim territory for Christ. The living wall of which we have spoken permits the Church to "claim a specific space for itself within the world, thus drawing a clear dividing line between itself and the world."[8]

---

[4]W. H. Auden, "City without Walls," *Collected Poems*, ed. Edward Mendelson (New York: Random House, 1976) 562-65.

[5]Dietrich Bonhoeffer, *Discipleship*, ed. and trans. from the German ed. of Bonhoeffer's *Works* (Minneapolis: Fortress, 2001) 4:225.

[6]Bonhoeffer, *Discipleship*, 232.

[7]Bonhoeffer, *Discipleship*, 244.

[8] Bonhoeffer, *Discipleship*, 261.

Today, in the mobile, uprooted culture spawned by urbanization and technology, our sense of community is rapidly eroding. Rampant individualism causes some to seek salvation by self-help and others to join the "invisible church" of the electronic media. But our passage makes clear that there is no substitute for the building up of a solid wall of humanity, drawn from every quarter, giving high visibility to the truth that, in Christ, enemies can be reconciled to God and to each other in the midst of their earthly existence. As Christian communities live out that unity and harmony in concrete fashion, their life together becomes a standing invitation to discover the secret of their unique solidarity, namely, the reconciling God—Father, Son, and Spirit—who lives within their midst. To accept such a God by faith is to participate directly in the reconciling process, for the person who becomes one with Christ also becomes one with all who belong to him.

(2) *To defend.* Walls protect our privacy from unwarranted intrusion. Imagine a bathroom or a laboratory or a prison without any walls! They provide safety for the vulnerable, offering protection to infants against the hazards beyond their door and to the aged against vandals who would molest. They guard our common treasures lest thieves break in to steal. What good is a bank or a museum or a jewelry store without sturdy walls?

Just so, the church, as a living wall, offers not only identity to those on the inside but security against threats from the outside. Because the holy God dwells within its midst, the New Temple and each of its members are to "shun immorality" (1 Cor. 6:18–20) and idolatry (2 Cor. 6:14–7:1). "For what *partnership* have righteousness and iniquity? Or what *fellowship* has light with darkness? What *accord* has

Christ with Belial? Or what has a believer in *common* with an unbeliever? What *agreement* has the temple of God with idols?" (2 Cor. 6:14–16). The same walls that unite those who are set apart as holy also separates them from all of those who are unclean (v. 17). At bottom, there is an ultimate difference between those who are "crucified with Christ" (Gal. 2:20) and those who "crucify… the Son of god afresh" (Heb. 6:6 KJV), and it is a necessary function of living walls to mark this difference.

In our permissive culture, this ethical note sounds harsh and unyielding, as if we were back to an exclusivism as rigid as any found in ancient Judaism. Essential differences must be noted, however. In the Jerusalem Temple, as we have seen, separation was based on factors of birth over which the individual had no control, such as whether born a Jew or Gentile, male or female, priest or layperson. But in the New Temple, separatism is based on a new birth by faith in which the individual is an active participant. Jesus made quite clear that uncleanness is not external but internal, not a matter of ancestry but of attitude, not an affair of the stomach but of the heart (Mk. 7:14-23). He described defilement in terms of evil thoughts from within that are no respecter of ethnic or sexual or vocational status.

To build a clear wall between the church and the world is not to claim that everyone on one side is perfect and that everyone on the other side is worthless. Such boasting would imply that salvation is by church affiliation instead of by God's grace. Obviously, there are unbelievers who have honored their humanity by accepting a high level of commitment to our common values; whereas, there are believers who have disgraced the gospel by falling far short of their spiritual potential. What the wall signifies is that those who "house" the Holy Spirit in their common life are seeking sanctification, not through self-help, but through a living relationship to the holiness of God. The wall, as it were, distances Christians from the spirit of this age, not in order to afford an escape from involvement with its plight, but as a reminder that they are to be *in* the world but not *of* it (Eph. 4:17-24).

(3) *To depict.* Precisely because walls define a reality, giving it identity and integrity, and because they defend that reality from compromise and corruption by outside forces, the walls themselves come to betoken that which they enclose. Thus, for example, the White House in Washington denotes the political leadership that is exercised within its walls. The Wailing Wall in Jerusalem signifies centuries of anguished longing for a Jewish homeland. The Berlin Wall, as long as it stood, pointed beyond itself to a totalitarianism that stifled freedom in Eastern Europe. In like manner, the living walls of a church stand for the religion that is practiced therein.

What does it portend when a miscellaneous assortment of folk who had been total "strangers" are fused into a solid phalanx of "fellow citizens" through the Spirit of Jesus Christ? Unlike other earthly walls, this living structure signifies far more than any human ideal of brotherhood, for ultimately it foreshadows the fellowship of heaven. In theological terms, the metaphor of the church as a spiritual sanctuary has not only ecclesiological and ethical but eschatological significance as well.

In the Judaism of this period, the establishment of the promised New Temple was viewed as a future event that would become a prominent feature of the messianic age.[9] For Paul to announce that such a structure was already under construction and growing toward completion, even though the Jerusalem Temple continued to stand on Mount Zion, was to imply that the New Age had already been inaugurated in the midst of the Old Age. The two temples overlapped just as the two ages overlapped (1 Cor. 10:11). The reconciliation of Gentile and Jew in one body anticipated the eternal plan of the ages "to unite all things" in Christ (Eph. 1:10).[10] And yet this transformation was taking place, not in apocalyptic splendor, but in obscure Christian communities founded by an apostle who was then in chains!

This scandal of the New Temple slipping unobtrusively into history, without any fanfare and at the most unlikely places, means that eternity comes not by divine fiat but wherever it finds human faith. The New Temple of reconciled lives can never be historicized as a permanent, visible institution. Every Christian congregation does not automatically show forth the profound unity with one another and with God depicted in Ephesians. No, it is only by faith that we allow the future to enter the present and eternity to shape the process of time. The New Temple never comes to earth because it is socially acceptable or politically expedient or economically advantageous but only because, by faith, persons dare to actualize the realities of the New Age amid the appearances of the Old Age. Such a temple is always

---

[9]The concept is mentioned in 1 Enoch 53:6; 90:28; 91:13; 2 Baruch 4:2-6; 6:7-8; 4 Ezra 7:26; Testament of Levi 5:1; Jubilees 1:29; Sibylline Oracles 5:414-433; Qumran 1QM 2:1-6; CD 6:2-11; 1QS 8:1-9:6; 9:10-11.

[10]Stig Hanson, *The Unity of the Church in the New Testament: Colossians and Ephesians* (Uppsala: Almqvist & Wiksells, 1946).

"ahead of the times" because it belongs to no time but, rather, foreshadows the worship "in spirit and truth" that "is coming, and is now here" (Jn. 4:23).

Robert Frost, in his familiar "Mending Wall,"[11] struggled with the subtle tension that this chapter seeks to resolve. The poem begins where this book began: "Something there is that doesn't love a wall, / That wants it down." But over against a yearning for openness and freedom is set the prudential wisdom handed down from the fathers: "Good fences make good neighbors." And so, "at spring mending-time," the neighbor comes to rebuild the gaps, "Bringing a stone grasped firmly by the top / In each hand, like an old-stone savage armed." Thus, the immemorial plot is set between our deep impulse to be rid of all walls and our equally deep instinct to keep them firmly in place.

By now we have come to realize that mirrored in that delicate dialectic is a central issue of human existence, namely, *how shall we deal with the structures that divide us*? Shall we dismantle them, ignore them, or reinforce them? Frost answered: "Before I built a wall I'd ask to know / What I was walling in or walling out, / And to whom I was like to give offense." That insight prepares us to understand and accept one central contention of our scriptural text: walls, as such, are not inherently good or bad; rather, they are bad when they function as walls of hostility and good when they clear a place for unity and peace to flourish.

If Robert Frost taught us to ask the right questions, then Jesus Christ supplied the right answers. In building the New

---

[11]Robert Frost, "Mending Wall," *The Poetry of Robert Frost*, ed. Edward Connery Lathem (New York: Holt, Rinehart and Winston, 1969) 33-34.

Temple, we must always "ask to know" what we are "walling in," and the answer of Ephesians 2:19-22 is that we are walling in ourselves with "fellow citizens" who together constitute a divine commonwealth set to oppose the "principalities and powers" of this world. We are walling in "the household of God," a spiritual family living in loving fellowship with one another. We are walling in the "dwelling place of God in the Spirit," the divine Presence on earth offered without measure to all who draw near. But we must also "ask to know" what we are "walling out," and here the answer of Ephesians 2:11-14 is that we are walling out spiritual elitism, alienation, and separatism that would keep at a distance any who are in union with Christ Jesus.

Paradoxically, then, Christ tears down our false human walls that divide in order to put in their place, true divine walls that unite. This means that the New Temple is designed to "wall in" those who are determined to live without barriers of hostility. The neighbor in Frost's poem was wrong. Good fences do *not* make good neighbors. Rather, the peace of Christ's cross makes good neighbors, for it is a peace that knows no boundaries, but invites strangers from far and near to become united "in one body."

To be sure, it is not easy to forge a fellowship in which all are equal before God. The dead weight of tradition, the power of prejudice, the tyranny of the status quo are all arrayed against us. But Christ has *already* broken down every barrier and has called us to live by faith in a community where there are no walls between us but where we are united into a living wall built out of all who join us. This kind of New Temple is to be found, not somewhere in heaven, but everywhere that God dwells among his people in the Spirit of Christ.

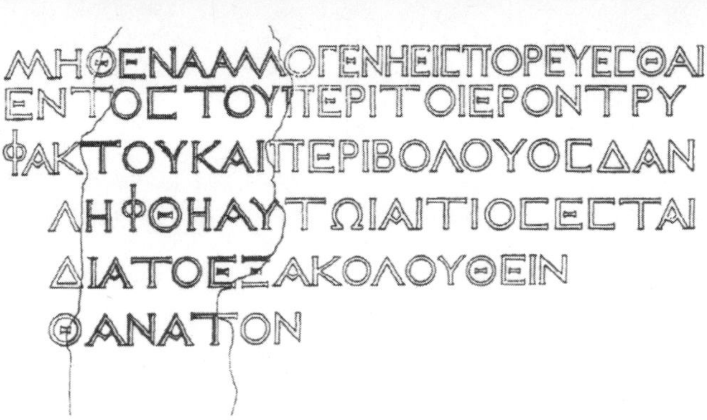

The inner enclosure wall (called the soreg) of the Herodian Temple complex separated the outer courts from the inner precincts into which only Jews were allowed. Signs suchas this one were posted, in Greek, at regualr intervals along the soreg, warning non-Jews not to enter, on penalty of death. The part of the sign that has been recovered is shaded in the reconstruction of the entire inscription below.

7

Controversy in the Church

A Personal Postscript

I conclude this study with a personal plea. First let me sketch the context out of which it comes. For sixty years (1950–2010) I ministered in the Baptist movement of the southern United States as a congregational pastor, seminary educator, and university administrator. Denominationally, I was related during half this time (1950–1980) to the Southern Baptist Convention (SBC), the other half (1980–2010) to what has become the Cooperative Baptist Fellowship (CBF). Theologically, I avoided labels as too limiting, but most informed observers would have described me as a Free Church moderate or centrist, which means that I sought to mediate between competing strands of the many-splendored Christian faith in the quest to achieve a reconciliation that had biblical integrity. As I began the move into retirement, I was stricken with a debilitating disease (ALS) that has forced me to curtail my physical activities, but these restrictions have freed me to reflect on the meaning of my ministry. Let me share with you some of what I have learned that prompted me to write this chapter.

I

The dominant challenge of my career has been to overcome controversy among Christians. With a decentralized ecclesiology, Baptists have never been good at maintaining church order. Indeed, their entire 400-year history has been marked by turmoil and travail. I should have been prepared to work in this climate of contention by my seminary training, but such was not the case either in the classroom or in the textbooks, presumably in an effort to minimize one of the more embarrassing features of Baptist life. Instead, I was left to jump into the fray and learn how to engage in religious warfare on my own, both to defend the way I was doing ministry and to protect those institutions that supported my approach. Here I identify the major controversies that dominated each decade of my ministerial career.

1950s. The upheaval of World War II thrust the US into the center of the global scene, challenging the isolationism so popular during the Depression years. As the Cold War divided East and West into hostile camps with competing ideologies, Baptists had to decide whether to go it alone in a self-sufficient separatism called Landmarkism or whether to enter into respectful dialogue with other denominations and world religions to search for areas of consensus, which was called ecumenism.

1960s. Launched by a Supreme Court ruling in 1954 and fueled by sweeping congressional legislation in 1964--1965, the civil rights struggle for equality and dignity, particularly by African-American citizens, dominated the entire decade. Southern Baptists had to decide whether to remain the most segregated major denomination in America or to open their doors to an increasingly diverse ethnic pluralism and share life freely with those whom they had long exploited.

1970s. The sexual revolution that had been building through the sixties, particularly in its "Woman's Lib" expression, came to an explosive climax in the Supreme Court's *Roe v. Wade* ruling of 1973. Through the efforts of independent churchmen such as Jerry Falwell, opposition to abortion for any reason became a test of evangelical orthodoxy. Baptists had to decide whether to adopt this absolutist position or whether to maintain their historic position that abortion could be permitted as a last resort in cases such as rape, incest, endangerment to the life of the mother, and fetal deformity so severe that the infant could not survive long after birth.[1]

1980s. Frustrated by their limited ability to influence public life on issues such as abortion, the most conservative

---

[1]In 1971, the SBC in annual session "adopted overwhelmingly" a resolution that called upon Southern Baptists "to work for legislation that will allow the possibility of abortion under such conditions as rape, incest, clear evidence of severe fetal deformity, and carefully ascertained evidence of the likelihood of damage to the emotional, mental, and physical health of the mother." In 1974, just after the *Roe v. Wade* ruling, the SBC acted to reaffirm the 1971 resolution that "reflected a middle ground between the extreme of abortion on demand and the opposite extreme of all abortion as murder." By 1976, a moderate resolution on abortion was again adopted but only after defeating two amendments, one declaring that "every decision for an abortion, for whatever reason, must necessarily involve the decision to terminate the life of an innocent human being;" and another claiming that "we reject, as contrary to Southern Baptist doctrine and tradition, any suggestion that Southern Baptists should become political activists in support of permissive legislation." *Annual of the Southern Baptist Convention* (Nashville: Executive Committee, SBC) 1971:72; 1974:73-76; 1976:57-58.

wing of Baptist life entered into a mutually acceptable agreement with Ronald Reagan's operatives according to which they would give him their unified support in his bid for the US presidency and, if elected, he would give their agenda his sympathetic support. Once this compact succeeded and Reagan's popularity soared, his Baptist sponsors attained enough legitimacy to banish moderates from positions of influence in the SBC by using the code word "inerrancy" as a test to identify supporters of the now regnant conservatism. This controversy was so momentous that it dominated not just a decade but an entire generation of SBC life. It forced Baptists to decide whether they would practice partisan politics to the point of block voting by aligning the denomination with one party and its prevailing ideology, or whether they would welcome those who accepted Christ as Lord regardless of their party affiliation or ideological persuasion.

1990s. The practice of biblical inerrancy proved to be a difficult test to apply in separating moderates from conservatives because it required the equivalent of a seminary education to understand the issues and to apply this approach to the interpretation of Scripture. Thus its advocates searched for a simple but significant practice on which churches were beginning to differ, and came up with the proper role of women in congregational leadership. Already in society, women were being admitted to top positions in higher education, the professions, business, government, and the military from which they had long been arbitrarily excluded by gender. Baptists had to decide whether to restrict women to their traditional church domains of kitchen, choir, and nursery, or whether to ordain them for wider service as deacons, pastors, and more specialized ministries such as chaplains.

2000s. Once the male superiority/female subordination pattern had been broken in many segments of society, both sexes felt empowered to relate to each other as equals. This leveling of gender distinctions, according to which couples comprised of both sexes were no longer needed to fulfill quite different functions, emboldened partners comprised of the same sex to come "out of the closet" and openly declare their homosexual orientation. Although they constituted a small percentage of the general population, gays and lesbians campaigned so vigorously for social acceptance and legal equality, particularly the right to marry, that they accomplished many of their goals in a few years. The widespread acceptance in the work place of a prohibition against discrimination for sexual orientation suggests that they will achieve even more of their goals in the near future. Already Baptists are having to decide whether to continue their strong denunciation of homosexuality or whether to be accepting, even affirming, when those who embrace this lifestyle seek membership in their churches.

II

At first glance, each of these controversies seems very different from the others, but underlying their diverse subject matter is a common pattern whose component parts I now describe somewhat in chronological order.

1. As hinted in the opening sentence of each entry in the list above, controversy tends to originate in the world rather than in the church, whether it be the rise of the Cold War, the seating policy of a Montgomery bus company, or the

availability of birth-control pills. Once some change provokes disagreement among influential opinion makers, it is seized upon by the media and turned into a fight-to-the-finish. By the time that a disputed agenda arouses the church, what may have begun as a friendly dialogue in an obscure seminar room now becomes a burning issue of compelling importance to be settled with urgency. Those Baptists who decide to belatedly address the problem have already been saturated with endless newspaper op-ed columns, television talk-shows, and computer blogs that prompt them to view the issue in adversarial terms.

Ministers, in particular, find it difficult to deal with the secularization of controversy by the media before it ever reaches them, primarily because they are accustomed to think in traditional theological categories. Most have little training in how to relate their religious frame of reference to the way in which the secular media shape the debate. The resulting clash of conceptual presuppositions almost inevitably prompts them to opt for the conservative choice and to see it as a spiritual battle to be won or lost.

This tendency was frequently impressed upon me when I led continuing education sessions involving ministers. As the conflicts referenced above were unfolding, I would probe their engagement with these issues by asking questions such as these. Did you ever

(1) attend an ecumenical meeting or serve on an interfaith dialogue group with another denomination or religion? (1950s);

(2) participate in a civil rights protest or talk to the leaders of such demonstrations? (1960s);

(3) discuss with one or more women who had undergone an abortion why they chose to terminate a pregnancy and what were the main aftereffects of their decision? (1970s);

(4) ask one or more candidates for public office on the Democratic ticket what they thought about the endorsement of Republican candidates by prominent Baptist leaders? (1980s);

(5) interview successful business and professional women in your church to determine their attitude toward being excluded from key boards and committees by reason of gender? (1990s);

(6) visit active church members whose sons or daughters were openly practicing gays or lesbians to learn their view on appropriate policies governing homosexual participation in your congregation? (2000s).

The most startling thing about this informal interrogation was the paucity of positive responses. Often in a group of fifty to a hundred pastors, none or only a handful would indicate that they had taken steps to learn at first hand both sides of the dominant controversy needing to be addressed. I do not offer these random samplings as a scientific survey, but I did gather this kind of feedback long enough (for more than fifty years) and widely enough (in most states of the Southeast), with results consistent enough (well under ten percent) to accept its validity.

Most modern Baptists, unlike their founders, have a bias against change. Faced with social upheaval they cling to the status quo, not bothering to examine the possibilities offered by new alternatives. This is not to say that the new is always, or even more often, better than the old. But it is to say that Baptists will never be able to make meaningful choices between the old and the new if they know only half the agenda. Mark it well: we fear, and then fight, that which is foreign to us.

2. Unfortunately, Baptists are ill-equipped to deal not only with controversies handed off to them from the world by the secular media but also with disputes that arise out of the life of its churches. If internal controversy is to dominate the way Baptists decide what they believe, as it has for many years, then this approach deserves careful preparation. Abundant resources were readily available but seldom consulted on all six of the disputes mentioned above.

For example, I served on the SBC Peace Committee (1985–1988) established to investigate and make recommendations to resolve tensions created by pastoral insurgents intent on replacing trustee incumbents in order to turn denominational agencies in a much more conservative direction. The tape recordings of our many sessions, all of which are now available, show that we never studied any of the standard literature on conflict resolution; or case studies of the way other denominations handled crises similar to ours, such as the Presbyterian and Northern Baptist denominations on their internal strife with fundamentalism in the twenties or the Lutheran Church, Missouri Synod over Concordia Seminary in the seventies. Indeed, we did not even consult the extensive material on inerrancy, the key rallying cry used to convince uninvolved Baptists that the takeover was theologically legitimate. Most amazing of all, we ignored our "sole rule of faith and order" by paying no attention to how the New Testament church dealt with its greatest conflict so much like ours. Lacking any biblical or historical frame of reference, the Committee soon became a microcosm of the Convention that had appointed it, endlessly rehashing pro and con arguments, like ammunition in a war, to determine who would be on the winning and losing sides.

Baptists have never been a studious people, excluded for more than half their history by the leading institutions of higher education in Europe, Great Britain, and America. As a result, they prefer to rely on personal experience and congregational consensus rather than on scholarly analysis and rational argumentation as sources of their deepest convictions. Regrettably, however, when embroiled in controversy, they abandon their traditional approaches that have served them well for an ad hoc shoot-from-the-hip approach that tends to favor authoritarian preachers accustomed to dominate discussion.

3. Because of the prominence of controversies in the secular media, they are given exaggerated importance in church life until resolved. For example, as regards the dominant disputes summarized above, I spent my ministry advocating an openness by Baptists

(1) to the whole worldwide church (1950s);

(2) to the acceptance of all Christians into the life of the congregation regardless of ethnicity or nationality (1960s);

(3) to those on both sides of the abortion question struggling to define a practice that honors God's will

as discerned by all involved in the birth process (1970s);

(4) to the findings of dedicated biblical scholars when their research clarifies or corrects uninformed views of both conservatives and liberals (1980s);

(5) to the full expression of gifts for church leadership by women as well as men (1990s);

(6) to heterosexuals and homosexuals alike without stigmatizing either group but ministering compassionately to the problems faced by both (2000s).

Because I adopted these positions, all of them embraced by well-informed segments of both society and the church, but not by many in my denomination, I spent almost my entire ministry wondering if the Baptist institutions in which I worked would be forced to fire me because of pressure from those holding contrary views. After all, many of my ministerial and academic colleagues were being unmercifully harassed and terminated for holding similar views, even though they embraced biblical faith, classic orthodoxy, and historic Baptist distinctives.

Religious controversy typically begins as an inadequate response to some contemporary issue. Sorting out the various options tends to oversimplify the problem, but this reductionism continues until there are only two sides that express the sharpest differences between the two positions. This very structure of the discussion turns into a win/lose struggle which, the longer it continues, degenerates into open warfare. Now there is no room for reconciliation, no concessions to be negotiated, no search for common ground. Instead, the conflict finally becomes a holy crusade to defend non-negotiable convictions in the name of God. When both sides absolutize their position by appealing to the Divine, their religious arguments cancel each other out, leaving the combatants to fight with the political weapons of the world in the hope that their cause will be victorious. Regardless of which side triumphs in that kind of dispute, one of the first casualties is a healthy tolerance of diversity.

4. We are now ready to face the irony in this destructive effort to reach a one-sided solution. After paying the fearful price of spreading dissention in the church, the victors in this so-called Holy War are seldom able to retain for long the spoils of their conquests, primarily because those on neither side of a controversy have a monopoly on truth. Slowly but surely, the wisdom embedded in the position of the losing side, and therefore repudiated in the heat of battle, eventually resurfaces to find expression in a more hospitable climate. Let us note the fortunes of the winning side in our six controversies after only a few years.

(1) In pursuing an isolationist course in the fifties, conservative Baptists made ecumenism a bad word but are now working closely with Evangelicals comprised of even more denominational backgrounds than the mainline ecumenical movement that they spurned.

(2) Most Southern Baptists followed the lead of demagogic Southern governors in the sixties and stood firm for segregation, then spent the years since then backtracking and publicly apologizing for their prejudices.

(3) In the seventies, Baptists took an aggressive posture on abortion that put them in the forefront of a crusade to overturn *Roe v. Wade* with a constitutional amendment but, presidential promises notwithstanding, such an initiative never went from Reagan to Congress.

(4) Southern Baptists put all of their eggs in the Republican basket in the eighties, only to discover before the decade was over that they could influence presidential elections far less than they had supposed. To their chagrin, they got as Reagan's successor not only a Democrat but a born-and-bred Southern Baptist who embarrassed them repeatedly by his sexual misadventures. So much for trying to unite rather than separate church and state!

(5) SBC Baptists took formal action in the nineties to deny church wide leadership roles to women, particularly the ordained ministry of senior pastor, because it would put them in authority over men, only to see women serve effectively as governors, senators, cabinet officers, and CEOs of vast corporations, which placed them in authority over thousands if not millions of men.

(6) It is too soon to learn how the hard line that most Southern Baptists are taking toward homosexuality in the new century will play out in the future, but already the condemnatory tone sounds harsh and unyielding to many observers as if Baptists want

nothing to do with gays despite the "hate the sin/love the sinner" explanations being offered.

To this point in our critique of contemporary religious controversy we seem to have concentrated exclusively on Baptists in the South, presumably because they have a reputation for internal bickering that is unsurpassed. That would be a mistaken perception, however, because all of the major denominations in the region have been convulsed with the same conflicts. Not only Baptists but Lutherans and Presbyterians have undergone major schisms over the inerrancy of Scripture. Catholics lead the way in squabbling over ministerial roles for women, while the Anglican communion is in tatters over the ordination of homosexuals as priests and bishops. One might suppose that such basic issues would have been settled by the church long ago but, if anything, the contested agenda is growing in scope and intensity as the years come and go. Furthermore, the sharpest invective is not directed against other denominations in competitive fashion, much as Baptists and Catholics used to feud simply because they were so different. Rather, by some perverse psychology, each group seems to derive the greatest satisfaction from castigating its closest spiritual kin.

This perpetual self-flagellation distracts Baptists in their need to learn from the successes and failures of other religious groups. Even more serious, by focusing their energies on fellow believers with whom they may differ on a few doctrines that the church has struggled for centuries to clarify, they take their eyes off the true enemies of the faith, allowing them to make havoc of our core convictions and leave the culture a spiritual wasteland. I have listened to Baptists shout at each other about real or imagined heresies but not manage a whisper of opposition to the upsurge of violence that drenches the earth with blood from such atrocities as wars, ethnic cleansings, political purges, and religious rioting. Again, as the rich get richer and the poor get poorer, how many Baptists speak for the countless millions who die each year of starvation for lack of food and disease for lack of medicine? Or against a consumerist culture that openly endorses a prodigal extravagance never more obscene than at Christmas and Easter? The list of mortal threats to our faith is endless, but the silence of a clear, united voice to challenge the creeping secularism that would destroy our faith is deafening.

At times, when I am in the mood of C. S. Lewis writing *The Screwtape Letters*,[2] I fantasize what it would be like to be on the opposite side as a sworn enemy of the Christian faith. Biblical Christianity is so radically different from the temper of our times that it would be easy for me to compile a list of strategies with which to attack our most basic beliefs, much as the New Atheists are doing today. But how, I wonder, would I win the South, so churched that it is often called the "Bible Belt"? Millions upon millions of Southerners gladly affirm their faith, more than sixteen million of them in the SBC alone. Tempted to give up against so mighty a foe, Screwtape whispers in my ear, "Don't worry, Wormwood, before those Baptists ever get to the field of battle, they will begin to debate how best to respond to your threat. Leave them alone long enough and they will take sides in a full-fledged controversy with walls constructed out of words to define who is on which side. Separated by these walls, they will not

---

[2]C. S. Lewis, *The Screwtape Letters* (New York: Macmillan, 1954).

only dilute their strength but become strangers to one another, and this strangeness will foster animosity, causing hostility to gather at the walls they have built. When that happens you will win because they will have defeated themselves."

III

We have learned from our analysis of religious controversy that it compromises the ability of the church to fulfill its mission in two ways. First, to return to the imagery of our primary text, internal disagreements create barriers separating Christians into competing camps who might otherwise be united in a common enterprise. Second, hostilities fester at such walls because those on one side feel excluded by those on the other side. As animosities multiply, a sense of disconnectedness or even remoteness feeds estrangement between those with inherited advantages who feel "near" and those without these favorable privileges who feel "far away" (Eph. 2:11-14). Somehow both groups need to experience equality of access to the blessings of Christ regardless of their religious differences prior to or after conversion.

What was the controversy that called forth our Ephesian passage on how Christ demolished the walls that generated hostility within the church?[3] The answer lies in the first verse and it is a strange one indeed. The world of the first century

---

[3]I have sought to recast this case study of the circumcision controversy into sermonic form. See William E. Hull, "The Struggle for a Global Faith," *Harbingers of Hope: Claiming God's Promises in Today's World* (Birmingham: Samford University Press, 2007) 285-95.

addressed by Ephesians was divided into two groups, Jews and non-Jews, the latter called "Gentiles." The key boundary marker separating the whole human race in this fashion was circumcision. So crucial was this practice to the Jews that they defined themselves as "the circumcised" and Gentiles as "the uncircumcised" (Eph. 2:11).[4] Listen to Daniel Boyarin, a Professor of Talmudic Culture, comment on the heart of what was at stake here for observant Jews:

> The true cultural issue dividing Christians from Jews by the second century was the significance of body filiation, membership in a kin-group, for religious life. As long as participation in the religious community is tied to those rites which are special, performed by and marked in the body, the religion remains an affair of a particular tribal group, "Israel in the flesh." The fraughtness of circumcision (almost obsession with it) of all of these people is not to be found in the difficulty of the rite to perform but in the way that it is the most complete sign of the connection of the Torah to the concrete body of Israel.[5]

---

[4]The terms "circumcised" and "uncircumcised" were not only descriptive but also derogatory. As regards the former, Gentiles ridiculed Jews for assigning so much religious importance to what pagans viewed as the mutilation of the male sexual organ (Eph. 1:11-15). As regards the latter, the Jews retaliated by referring to Gentiles as "foreskins," a contrast obscured by the customary translation ("uncircumcised"). In other words, both epithets were insulting caricatures that Jews and Gentiles hurled at each other, which means that the "hostility" in v. 14, already bristled in the opening v. 11. See Joel Marcus, "The Circumcised and the Uncircumcised in Rome," *New Testament Studies* 35/1 (1989): 77-80.

[5]Daniel Boyarin, *A Radical Jew: Paul and the Politics of Identity*, (Berkeley: University of California Press, 1994), 36.

And yet Paul, a circumcised Jew, was quick to point out that the rite itself was merely something done to a bit of flesh by human hands (Eph. 2:11). We could add other limitations. The procedure itself seemed hardly to be a self-evident religious act. Moreover, it was gender specific, excluding the female half of the population. Even male circumcision was not unique to Judaism, being practiced throughout the Middle East, such as in nearby Egypt. Its religious roots in Israelite religion were sketchy at best, the Hebrew Bible recording its origin in the covenant with Abraham (Gen. 17:9-14) but not treating it anything like as fully as Temple worship or Sabbath observance. Today, non-Jews view circumcision as an elective surgical procedure without any religious significance. It is seldom mentioned in a church setting, not only because of the inherent delicacy of the subject matter, but because it does not seem to speak to our spiritual needs in any meaningful fashion.

But before we dismiss the subject out of hand, remember that circumcision was the most explosive issue in Paul's pivotal letter to the Galatians (2:3-9; 2:11-13; 5:1-12; 6:12-15) and that it recurred as a key theme in several of his later epistles as well (1 Cor. 7:17-19; Rom. 2:25-29; 3:30; 4:9-12; Phil. 3:2-3; Col. 2:11; 3:11; Eph. 2:11-13; Titus 1:10) Moreover, it was the central controversy prompting the Jerusalem Conference of Acts 15, which became, in many ways, the watershed event of the apostolic era. Somehow we need to discover why this peculiar religious practice became the first and, for a time, the most important controversy to confront the early church.

The New Testament period was a time of escalating tensions between Judaism and its enemies. Palestine had been culturally conquered by the Greeks and militarily conquered by the Romans. As a result, Jews everywhere felt threatened with assimilation into the foreign culture of the Mediterranean world that would cause their distinctive way of life to disappear. Many of the religious leaders in Palestine, alarmed by what they viewed as the increasing power of a secular culture, began to practice the politics of polarization, that eventually erupted in a futile fight to the finish against the mighty Roman Empire. The Jewish war of AD 66--73 resulted in the fall of Jerusalem, the destruction of the Temple, and the loss of a homeland in Palestine.

Since, in the ancient struggle for survival, the Jews had no flag around which to rally, they made circumcision the symbol of their embattled identity. Far from being an optional hygienic technique, the practice of circumcision as a religious symbol became the dividing line that separated Jews from the rest of the world. Its decisive importance in first-century Judaism is seen clearly in *Jubilees* 15.26 from that era:

> And anyone who is born whose own flesh is not circumcised on the eighth day is not from the sons of the covenant which the Lord made for Abraham since (he is) from the children of destruction. And there is therefore no sign upon him so that he might belong to the Lord because [he is destined] to be destroyed and annihilated from the earth and to be uprooted from the earth because he has broken the covenant of the Lord our God.[6]

---

[6]James H. Charlesworth, ed., *The Old Testament Pseudepigrapha* (Garden City NY: Doubleday, 1985) 2:87.

Aware of the sacred significance that the Jews attached to circumcision, their Greek and Roman masters pressured them relentlessly to renounce what they viewed as a repugnant practice (1 Macc. 1:14-15). Efforts to remove its mark by surgery became common among the urban upper class of Jews and was viewed by the historian Josephus as forsaking Jewish customs to adopt a Greek way of life (*Jewish Antiquities* 12.241). Those who refused to repudiate circumcision were ostracized from the gymnasium, the public bath, and the athletic contests, all of which involved only males who participated in the nude. In some instances, the defiant practice of circumcision could lead to punitive taxation, loss of citizenship, or even death, as when Antiochus IV Epiphanes slaughtered those families who circumcised their children and hung the infants from their mother's necks (1 Macc. 1:60-61; 2 Macc. 6:10). By the time that Paul began his missionary work around AD 50, circumcision had become the battle cry of patriotic Jews determined to avoid extinction as God's chosen people in a pagan culture.

Paul had been born and raised as an observant Jew, "circumcised on the eighth day" (Phil. 3:5). As we know from Romans 9-11, his heart's deepest desire was to win his fellow countrymen (Rom. 10:1). Therefore, he was willing for Timothy to be circumcised to facilitate his acceptance by Jews in their synagogues (Acts 16:3), but he adamantly refused to require it of Titus, a Greek who would work primarily with Gentiles (Gal. 2:3). He knew that most non-Jews would never accept his gospel message on condition of circumcision, because it would entangle them in a cultural and political controversy with which they wanted no part. This does not mean that Paul simply abandoned a practice clearly taught in his Hebrew Bible. Rather, he had learned from the martyr

Stephen that the Abrahamic covenant of circumcision (Acts 7:8) failed to circumcise the heart and ears of the people, causing them to resist the Holy Spirit and reject God's messengers (Acts 7:51-53). Rather than repudiating circumcision, Paul internalized its meaning so that his Christianity would become a religion of the spirit, rather than of the flesh (Col. 2:11-13).

His bold strategy of eliminating circumcision from his gospel to the Gentiles was bound to result in open conflict with Jews (Gal. 2:4-5), for it raised the broader issue of what practices in Judaism one had to embrace in order to become a Christian. The first effort to address this problem resulted in a "two-spheres" solution according to which there would be dual strategies, a mission to circumcised Jews led by Peter and a mission to uncircumcised Gentiles led by Paul (Gal. 2:7-9). Again and again, Paul tried to honor this compromise in evenhanded fashion (1 Cor. 7:18-19). After all, his driving passion was to win as many as possible, regardless of whether they were Jew or Gentile (1 Cor. 9:19-22).

For a brief time this approach seemed to succeed as Christianity flourished, not only in Paul's Gentile churches, but in the Jerusalem church led by James where "many thousands . . . among the Jews," who were "all zealous for the law," had become believers (Acts 21:20). The solution seemed fair to all. Gentiles did not have to become Jews in order to become Christians, nor did Jews have to become Gentiles in order to become Christians. It was to be a win/win solution for those on both sides of the issue.

Soon this strategy began to fail, however, precisely because of its success, when a growing number of Jewish Christians and Gentile Christians began to mingle in cosmopolitan centers, such as Antioch. The reason for its failure was that a small but fanatical group within the church called Judaizers refused to accept the "two-spheres" accommodation but insisted that every Christian obey the ancestral customs of the Jews as set forth in Scripture. These Judaizers organized themselves into "the circumcision party" and pressured Peter to stop eating with Gentile Christians in Antioch because they were not circumcised and did not observe kosher food requirements. In yielding to their pressure, Peter incurred the wrath of Paul who "opposed him to his face, because he stood self-condemned" (Gal. 2:11-12). By insisting on their understanding of the *purity* of the church, which involved a literalistic observance of such Old Testament practices as circumcision, the Judaizers were disrupting the *unity* of the church at the crucial point of table fellowship, which included the Lord's Supper.

As political and cultural tensions rapidly escalated in Palestine, the Judaizers increased their agitation by insisting that circumcision was essential to salvation (Acts 15:1). When this led to "no small dissension and debate" (Acts 15:2), it was decided to convene a summit which we call the Jerusalem Conference. Included among the participants was a party of Pharisaic believers determined to prevail on the issue of circumcision by demanding that all Christians be "ordered to keep the law of Moses" (Acts 15:5). As the debate unfolded, both Peter and James sided with Barnabus and Paul, emphasizing that salvation was only "through the grace of the Lord Jesus" (v. 11), and, therefore, Jewish requirements should not be imposed upon "those Gentiles who are turning to God" (Acts 15:19 NRSV). A diplomatically worded apostolic decree was drawn up urging each side to be respectful of the religious scruples of the other side as shaped by custom and culture, but not to allow these human differences to impede anyone from accepting Christ (Acts 15:22-29).

With all of the key leaders in agreement, it might seem that the matter had finally been settled, but such was not the case. The next time that Paul returned to Jerusalem, he found a powder keg of political extremism ready to explode. Even his willingness to demonstrate loyalty to Jewish religious customs did nothing to abate the tension (Acts 21:17-28). Instead, the inflammatory attitude resulted in him almost being lynched in the shadow of the Sanctuary as the result of the merest suspicion that he might have taken a Gentile, Trophimus the Ephesian, into the Temple (Acts 21:27-32). Paul's life was spared by the intervention of Roman soldiers, but the rest of his ministry was spent as a prisoner processing judicial appeals to ever higher levels of the Roman government.

No wonder he became so frustrated over the circumcision issue that, in exasperation, he invited those who were demanding the circumcision of Gentiles apply the knife to themselves and be castrated (Gal. 5:12)! Paul washed his hands of the issue by insisting that physical circumcision simply did not matter to the Christian faith despite the claims of his detractors (Gal. 5:6; 6:15). After his death, the issue was finally settled, not by apostolic summitry, but by Roman armies that brutally crushed a suicidal uprising of Jews fomented by the kind of religious dogmatism that had tried to wreck Paul's ministry.

What are some of the relevant lessons to be learned from the way the New Testament church handled this major controversy? The first is that Christianity is not an otherworldly escapist religion but one that addresses persons in their own distinctive setting and seeks to become indigenous in that culture as far as possible. Because of its rootedness in the real world of time and place, earthly pressures on the faith can become enormous. Particularly potent is the combination of patriotism and piety that seeks to make the church an agent of some group's political agenda. Religious people take seriously their earthly citizenship as well as their ethnic identity, and they desire to be loyal to their inherited traditions. In Jewish Christianity, this led to the emergence of a "circumcision party;" whereas, in our country it has resulted in a strong tradition of exclusivism with its frequently violent expressions of hostility to anything foreign. Sad to say, religion has often been in the forefront of strident efforts to sanctify sameness and demonize differences, but the early church resisted this disastrous temptation.

Second, in light of our enormous cultural diversity, it is not only legitimate but often necessary to have multiple strategies for resolving a controversy. In the New Testament era, this required one approach to Jews and another to Gentiles; whereas, today it may require different approaches to the First World and the Third World, or to the older generation and the younger generation, or to liberals and conservatives. In the twenty-first century as in the first century, we still have bitter "culture wars" that divide our nation into opposing camps with the antagonisms between them accentuated by the mass media. The remarkable thing is that, no matter how diverse we become, the spirit of Christ has a universal appeal to all groups regardless of their nationality, gender, political persuasion, or ideological preference.

Third, when we seek to resolve the tension between the particularity of our religious customs and the universality of our risen Lord, doctrinaire extremists can wreak havoc and subvert the worldwide outreach of the Christian faith regardless of the solutions we devise. In the ancient conflict over circumcision, everyone was not right. Even though the Book of Acts embraced a wide spectrum of opinion that included Stephen on the far left, Paul on the near left, Barnabas in the center, Peter on the near right, and James on the far right, this tolerance did not extend to the Judaizers who, by their inflexible absolutism, were splitting the church and hindering its world mission. We may assume that the Judaizers were trying to be sincere Christians but, judged by the verdict of history, they were deeply misguided in their nonnegotiable demands.

Fourth, when an irreconcilable impasse is reached, that does not mean that we throw up our hands in despair. Rather, our only choice is not between the two sides in whatever culture war is raging. We need not be stymied if various Christian groups reach a point where they cannot reconcile their differences. Our faith stands or falls, not on our ability to solve all of the problems presented by our diverse backgrounds, but on the ability of Christ himself to redeem those of every background. Only God is the providential Lord of history who can use even our disagreements to accomplish his will (Acts 21:14).

IV

It is now abundantly clear that religious controversy is a prime way to build walls of hostility within the church. Therefore, Christians must do everything possible to resolve such conflicts lest they divide and destroy the fellowship that undergirds our unity in Christ. Utilizing the principles discovered in our case study of circumcision, let us explore how the handling of that dispute might guide us to deal more constructively with the animosities that fester within our congregations today. I mention four imperatives that are especially important in that regard.

1. *Reorder priorities.* In discussing how Christ overcame the hostility between Jews and Gentiles, Paul explained that this involved not only their unification in one body but also their reconciliation in that body to God (Eph. 2:16). In so doing, he reflected a new and different understanding of reconciliation discussed more fully in 2 Corinthians 5:18-20. In the ancient world, religion was primarily a matter of appeasing the deity so that he would be reconciled to the worshipers. Paul stood that concept on its head by emphasizing that God took the initiative in reconciling us to himself (2 Cor. 5:18a). Furthermore, ancient worshippers limited this desire for reconciliation to themselves and those whom they cared about, whereas Paul emphasized that God had reconciled the whole of humanity to himself regardless of how many trespasses they had committed (2 Cor. 5:19).

Paul then used these claims to define every Christian's calling. In order that everyone might know what God had done for them, God gave us "the ministry of reconciliation" which includes "the message of reconciliation" (2 Corinthians 5:18-19). So exalted is this twofold commission that in fulfilling it we become "ambassadors for Christ" (v. 20) thereby identifying reconciliation as the most important work that we can do for him. To say that, as we "entreat," God is making his "appeal" means that this work should be the overriding passion of our hearts as it is of God's heart (2 Cor. 5:20). To put it simply, Paul spent his life primarily as a reconciler because his God and Christ his Lord were the ultimate reconcilers.

The scope of his efforts were staggering indeed. Using the concept of newness, Paul summarized some of his areas of involvement in a formula of before-and-after contrasts. Now there was neither Jew nor Greek, slave nor free, male nor female, circumcision nor uncircumcision, for they were all one in Christ Jesus (Gal. 3:28; 1 Cor. 12:13; Col. 3:11). The fact that such formulae were related to baptism (Gal. 3:27; 1 Cor. 12:13; Col. 3:9-10) may suggest that converts in any of these contrasting categories were equally welcome in the Christian community because their new identity "in Christ" transcended their inherited identity determined by nationality ethnicity, gender, and social standing. To be sure, earthly distinctions did not disappear, as if the end of the world had come, but the Spirit of Christ in their lives caused them to look at each person as a "new creation" that God intended them to become (2 Cor. 5:17).

In light of the Pauline concept of ministry, surely one of the most profound in Scripture, we must ask, where are our reconcilers today? The prevalence of deliberately provoked controversy, particularly in the church by its clergy, might prompt one to suppose that they feel called to a ministry of polarization rather than to one of reconciliation! Think of the many preachers who have earned a reputation for fearless courage when all they have done is use the immunity of the pulpit to bash their fellow clergy on some point of disagreement, often caused by nothing more than a lack of understanding. Instead, to return to the imagery of Ephesians, Christians must ask themselves, Am I building walls that will generate hostility because I chose to stand on one side in such a way that those with whom I differ are left standing on the other side? Or am I willing to become an integral part of the wall that God is building out of those who achieve true community by sharing the spirit of Christ?

To reorder our priorities will require not only a new emphasis but a comprehensive culture change rooted in a fresh realization of the oneness of God (Deut. 6:4; 1 Cor. 8:6). We are used to calling this monotheism and thinking it means that there are no rival deities competing with our Lord. While this understanding is true as far as it goes, the New Testament approach is quite different. There, God's oneness refers to how he relates to the world. It asserts that he does not deal with his creation in piecemeal or fragmentary fashion but, true to his nature, in organic or holistic fashion. Notice how God's oneness found expression in our key passage (Eph. 2): He did not act on the spur of the moment but "at *one* time" (v. 11) when he could make both Jews and Gentiles "into *one*" (v. 14) by sending Christ that "he might create in himself *one* new humanity" (v. 15). He did this by reconciling "both groups to God in *one* body" (v. 16) and by granting "access in *one* Spirit to the Father" (v. 18).

This singular concentration on how God acts in only one way for everybody despite their differences expresses two powerful truths greatly in need of being rediscovered.

First, it declares that central to God's will for planet earth is a desire to reconcile the estranged, unite the separated, and welcome the excluded in ways that honor their manifold diversity. The purpose of God in seeking a oneness on earth like unto his own oneness in heaven is to replace hostility (Eph. 2:14, 16) with peace (Eph. 2:14-15, 17) because he is "the God of peace" (Phil. 4:9, 1 Thess. 5:23; Heb. 13:20). By attaching the concept of peace through oneness to almost every aspect of the Christian faith, God has provided numerous reminders of what every Christian is to be about. Ministers in particular, should evaluate their leadership by the test of whether they are contributing to hostility or to peace within the household of God.

Second, the oneness of God's salvation on our behalf is designed to prevent anyone from taking sides over what he has done for them in comparison to others. In Ephesians 4:4-6, Paul applies a list of God's unique gifts to maintaining "the *unity* of the Spirit in the bond of *peace*" (Eph. 4:3). Since they are seven in number, we may take them as representing the typical way that God deals with us. Note that the thing they all have in common is oneness.

There is (1) *one* body and (2) *one* Spirit, just as you were called to the (3) *one* hope of your calling, (4) *one* Lord, (5) *one* faith, (6) *one* baptism, (7) *one* God and Father of all, who is above all and through all and in all.

There is a paradox at the heart of this passage that we have encountered before. On the one hand the relentless repetition of the sevenfold "one" makes it seem that God is rationing his blessings to a select few. Is just one of each adequate for our incredibly diverse world, or even for the Mediterranean world of Paul's day? And yet the passage comes to a ringing climax with the fourfold repetition of "all" (Eph. 4:6) The multidimensional "*of* all / *above* all / *through* all / *in* all" is designed to emphasize inclusiveness. Nobody could possibly be excluded from the blessings of a God who is everywhere! But look what this "one-for-all" formula does to our assigned ministry of reconciliation. Far from containing any contradiction, the divine arithmetic expressed in the formula makes the unity of God's people a necessity. For if there really is only one Savior (1 Tim. 2:5), and therefore only one gospel (Gal. 3:7), where would those whom we ostracize turn for redemption? If the answer be given that they could go out and start a church of their own where God might try to correct their false views, we are forced to confront the fact that there is just one body, one faith, and one baptism.

"One for all." How simple yet profound! Clearly this formula lies at the bedrock of the biblical understanding of how God relates to his world. But does it also inform our highest priorities for ministry? More than anything else, ministers are to be godly, and here we have a classic expression of this pattern of godliness: serving humanity without discrimination in such a way that "all" are united by sharing the "one" and only way that God has provided for those who follow Christ for salvation. Only when the fulfillment of this pattern becomes the plea of our prayers, the passion of our preaching, and the priority of our church programs, will our preoccupation with controversy begin to abate and our fratricidal hostility be replaced by the peace of God.

2. *Welcome Diversity.* This strong emphasis on the oneness of God and his people does not mean that all Christians are to be exactly alike. Diversity is obviously dominant in nature, scientists still cataloguing thousands of plant and animal species. Humanity is even more diverse, countless billions having lived on earth with each of them different in more ways than we can number. We may be sure that Paul encountered even more diversity than we do because he established churches across many cultures, each with their own history, traditions, and customs. While he waited for his immature converts to grow spiritually, Paul had to develop a strategy to keep them from splitting over nonessentials, as his correspondence with the Corinthian church vividly illustrates.

His strategy involved three components: (a) Cordiality, a Christian doctrine of tolerance that went beyond enduring each other to a warm acceptance that welcomed each other. (b) Conscience, a Christian doctrine of integrity that respected the differing views of all sides. (c) Compromise, a Christian doctrine of expediency that worked out a practical accommodation to implement God's plan of reconciliation. These three doctrines are not prominent in our discussion today, but they hold out our best hope of working together in united fashion. Let us explain each of these in turn.[7]

(1) *Cordiality*. As we saw in our case study of the circumcision controversy, Paul began as an implacable foe of the Judaizers, and retained hostility toward their extreme legalism to the end of his life. In the first fury of pastoral exasperation over the "stealing" of his Galatian converts, Paul hurled anathemas that made him seem intolerant (Gal. 1:6-9). But the longer Paul ministered, the clearer he saw that a solution must be devised to deal with mounting tensions between Jewish and Gentile Christians, especially in the politically turbulent decade of the mid-fifties to the mid-sixties.

The most mature expression of Paul's solution is found in Romans 14:1–15:13. The antagonists were labeled here as the "weak" and the "strong." These terms were used by the larger Gentile Christian group to define themselves as "strong" enough to defy traditional scruples in the Jewish law

---

[7]Robert Jewett, *Christian Tolerance: Paul's Message to the Modern Church* (Philadelphia: Westminster Press, 1982) has contributed helpfully to this section of our study. See also his more recent Hermeneia commentary on the key passage: *Romans: A Commentary* (Minneapolis: Fortress Press, 2007) 858-99.

such as dietary regulations, while the Jewish Christians were stigmatized as "weak" because they felt the need to maintain liturgical and ascetic practices from the past. To be sure, the "weak" were anything but that in holding to their convictions, some apparently condemning the "strong" for not even living up to the standards of those they called "weak."

To these feuding factions Paul called for cordiality in their relationships (Rom. 14:1; 15:7). From AD 49 to 54 in Rome the two groups had been growing apart, whereas they needed a depth of fellowship that would end hostile competition and affirm the legitimacy of both sides in the controversy. The basis of such acceptance was the gracious welcome of Christ. How dare they despise those whom Christ was willing to save? When we treat people as Christ treats them, then God is glorified.

Note that neither side was asked to change, nor did one side win while the other side lost. Paul advocated mutual tolerance, not the formal tolerance of unconcern but the positive or intrinsic tolerance that acknowledged both positions as valid because they were based on genuine encounters with the Divine. This kind of tolerance was not based on truth as rational correctness but on truth as experienced reality, a lived encounter with transcendence when Christ welcomed each of them. To "welcome" fellow Christians was not merely to respect their position as outsiders. Rather, it was to reach out in love and make them insiders. It says: I want you in the same way that Christ wanted you—just as you are!

Paul's solution was not based on moral relativism, as if the views of the two sides did not matter. Nor on a pragmatic adjustment to pluralistic reality, as if we should get together merely for the sake of togetherness. Nor on some lofty philosophical ideal about the unity of humankind, as civic or political solutions might emphasize. Rather, it was based on the saving work of God in human life: "as Christ has welcomed you" (Rom. 15:7). Here, in other words, was a Christocentric doctrine of tolerance built squarely on the theology of Romans 1--8. What it says in essence is that the only way that we can give glory to God is to be as tolerant as the God who sent Christ to welcome us home. The cordiality that overcomes hostility in a shared experience of divine grace.

(2) *Conscience*. But what does this kind of tolerance do to the autonomy of conscience that has played such a crucial role in American and Baptist history? Do we not defend one's liberty of conscience, even if mistaken? Then how do we deal with those who talk of opposing views as "theologically repugnant to conscience" and assume that "matters of conscience" are nonnegotiable? Some even set cordiality and conscience in tension, viewing tolerance as a liberal virtue and integrity as a conservative virtue. But Paul championed both in the same passage (Rom. 14:1–15:13).

He began by defending the autonomy both of the "weak" conscience and of the "strong" conscience because conscience is the guardian of one's personal integrity. To disregard conscience is the first step toward fragmenting the self (1 Cor. 8–10). Each side desired uniformity by forcing their convictions on the other side, but Paul urged both parties to remain true to their convictions (Rom. 14:22-23) but not to coerce the conscience of those with whom they differed.

He took this position because tolerance and integrity are both necessary to a balanced Christian life. To have tolerance without integrity leads to relativism, while to have integrity without tolerance leads to dogmatism. We achieve balance by being exclusively loyal to the one true God (integrity) without allowing any human constraints to limit our response to God (tolerance). When conscience is protected by tolerance, it leads to a healthy pluralism. Paul insisted that each individual be "fully convinced in his own mind" (Rom. 14:5). Nothing could more decisively sanction differing viewpoints. He did not say to conform to a majority position, or to yield to some authoritative leader, but to make up your own mind, which could result in an unlimited number of possibilities. The very nature of faith as something to be kept "as your own conviction before God" provides the basis for diversity of theological perspectives which produces growth on both sides in their search for a fresh consensus.

Of course pluralism can become dangerous when it becomes like relativism without any limits, nor did Paul teach a tolerance that knew no boundaries. For example, he spoke of "hating what is evil" and "holding fast to what is good" (Rom. 12:9). This implies that there are areas of moral and spiritual reality in which right and wrong are perfectly obvious. In such cases, a strong, consistent response is urged: "abhor evil, cleave to what is good." It is not inconsistent to be utterly intolerant of that which destroys tolerance. So Paul moved at two levels: the black and white level where issues are clearly drawn (Rom. 12:9-21) and the grey level where issues are ambiguous (Rom. 14:1–15:13). Which leaves us with the question of when compromise is permissible.

(3) *Compromise*. The great test case of Paul's life was the Jerusalem Conference of Acts 15 that we cited in our case study of the circumcision controversy. The issue was clear and simple: circumcision was clearly taught in the Bible and clearly honored for centuries of Jewish tradition. Even though

Gentiles who became Jewish proselytes were circumcised in adulthood, Paul did not require it of Christian converts who were Gentile. He knew that it was offensive to most Gentiles and thus a major hindrance to their conversion. Moreover, it was not intrinsically "good" or "evil" but only symbolic, something "made in the Flesh by human hands" (Eph. 2:11). Theologically, it was offensive to Paul as a form of legalism (Gal. 5:1-12), while its elimination by Paul was offensive to the Judaizers.

The solution reached in Jerusalem had three parts. (a) The necessity of circumcision for Gentiles was dropped. The Judaizers were defeated, yet nothing was said about this. (b) Barnabas and Paul, objects of severe criticism, were openly commended (Acts 15:25-26), thus enhancing their ability to serve. (c) Jewish-Gentile fellowship was strengthened by requests not to offend traditional Jewish sensibilities (Acts 15:20, 29; 21:25). Both could come to Christ in their respective cultures, yet each must respect the cultural differences of the other (Acts 15:8-9, 11).

On the one hand this solution defused an explosive controversy that threatened fellowship. It gave new impetus to mission. It asked only for symbolic rather than substantive concessions, yet stressed the importance of showing tender concern for each other. On the other hand, it did require compromise by both sides. Nobody got all that they wanted whether it be a Christianity bound to Judaism or a Christianity free of Judaism. Further, the solution was transitional. We hear almost nothing more of it in the rest of the New Testament or in early Christian literature. History soon swept the solution aside after it had made a useful contribution for its day.

Two things are clear from the Pauline strategy: there are inescapable differences that divide us and there are inescapable similarities that unite us. To be specific, we are bound to have different histories, traditions, and cultures, but similar spirit, purpose, and devotion. The good news is that we do not have to give up any of our differences as long as they do not interfere with our similarities. At its best, controversy is the sifting process by which we determine what diversity may be retained without endangering our unity in Christ. So let us with our apostolic forebears, learn to live together in loving tolerance and integrity of conscience by creative compromises that enable our mission of winning the world to go forward in unity and peace.

3. *Attempt the Impossible.* I have been working on this book for just over two years. As I dug more deeply into the subject matter, I increased my dialogue with leading pastors, educators, and denominational administrators regarding the feasibility of moving beyond the type of destructive controversies in which Baptists of the South seem to be perpetually engaged. Almost without exception their response was that any progress in this area is impossible, particularly as regards the "civil war" of 1979–1990 that split the SBC root and branch. The leading reason given was that the constituency was not ready for such an initiative, which made it impossible to lead a process of change in the voluntaristic decentralized Baptist tradition.

Even more disconcerting was the prevailing attitude that alienation is preferable to reconciliation. In the great controversy of the 1980s the two sides, when polite, referred to each other as conservatives and moderates, or, when angry, as fundamentalists and liberals. Both groups are well represented throughout the South, thus a denomination striving to reach that region should be equally well represented in its leadership by those able to present the Christian faith from both perspectives. But all I heard in my inquiries of either side was how nice it is to be rid of the other side. Now we can associate only with our own kind. Now we can believe what we want to without the other side trying to correct our distortions or balance our one-sided emphases. Now we can send a clear signal to prospects in the religious marketplace, even though it will not be for everybody but only for those who share our ideological bias.

Bottom line for all of this free advice was: Don't rock the boat! The winners emphasized keeping the status quo because they wanted to enjoy the fruits of their victory, the losers because they wanted to protect the fragile structures that they had developed in exile. Both sides agreed that this fracas had finally settled down and should not be disturbed. Once this input was clear and consistent, I decided to test it by the biblical witness. The circumcision controversy is particularly relevant in that regard both because we have already examined it in some detail and because it was a controversy that seemed to have been decisively settled at the highest level only to come apart in ways that Paul felt demanded his personal response. We look first at the evidence presented by the Book of Acts.

The Jerusalem Conference led by Peter (15:6-11), Barnabas (15:12), Paul (15:12), and James (15:13-21), resulted in a consensus supported by "the apostles and the elders, with the consent of the whole church" (15:22) that Gentiles not be required to undergo circumcision in order to become Christian. Even though this pivotal decision was widely shared with the churches (15:22-35), and Paul was able to resume his Gentile mission with great success (16:4-5), there are hints in the record that the circumcision problem was far from settled (20:22). The Judaizers, whose views had been rejected at the Jerusalem Conference, were hounding Paul's footsteps, demanding that his converts practice circumcision, an insistence supported by both Scripture and tradition. Their influence was nearing a climax because a powerful political movement within Judaism was urging an all-out war with Rome to defend and preserve Jewish distinctives. In light of these circumstances, Paul decided that a trip was necessary, not only to Jerusalem in an effort to save the Christian faith from Jewish legalism, but also to Rome in an effort to save it from being viewed as a revolutionary movement (19:21).

The record in Acts of Paul's final journey to Jerusalem is reminiscent of Jesus' last visit to the Holy City as recorded in the Synoptic Gospels. Both accounts emphasize a sense of foreboding that the trip would end in tragedy (21:13). Somewhat parallel to the three passion predictions by Jesus in the Synoptic Gospels (Mk. 8:31; 9:31; 10:33-35) are three sorrowful pleas to Paul by leaders of the churches at Ephesus (20:37), Tyre (21:4-5), and Caesarea (2:11-12) begging him to turn back. Sure enough, just as predicted, on reaching Jerusalem Paul found many thousands of Jewish Christians zealous for the Law who had been told that he was teaching Jews "to forsake Moses" by telling them "not to circumcise their children or observe the customs" (21:21). Nothing could have been more inflammatory or farther from the truth! The crowd quickly became a mob ready to riot (21:35). So confused were they by rumors and gossip (21:34) that all they wanted was to get rid of Paul without even the benefit of a trial (21:36). At this point the Roman occupation army had to intervene, if only to restore public order and somewhat unwittingly help Paul fulfill his wish to visit Rome.

The lessons of this biblical episode are not difficult to identify.

(1) Controversies settled top-down by respected leaders may come apart by bottom-up volatility at the grassroots level. In this case, political passions were fed by fear of assimilation into Greco-Roman culture, thus losing a distinctive identity cultivated for more than a thousand years and widely assumed within Judaism as essential for its survival.

(2) Controversies over important issues that resist settlement deserve a second effort that may be more difficult than the first. The circumcision agenda was utterly crucial to Paul because it would determine the fate of his Gentile mission. Therefore he was willing to risk anything, even his life, to have it settled in favor of a universal gospel.

(3) Controversial positions do not require majority support and a favorable climate before they may be addressed. Paul picked the worst possible time to reopen the circumcision question. Every church he visited was so strongly opposed to his strategy that they were certain it was not the will of God. Jewish Christians against Paul greatly outnumbered Gentile Christians for Paul. Clearly it was a hopeless situation, but what if Paul had not gone, leaving the Judaizers to win by default? He was only one against thousands, yet it takes only one to expose the weakness of a multitude, to define an alternative worthy of reflection by sober minds, and to plant a banner under which brave hearts could rally in better times.

(4) Controversies are better settled for the long-term future than for the short-term present. It is obvious that Paul's second effort to settle the circumcision controversy was a complete failure in any practical way. The exact date of his

death is uncertain, but it is likely that he went to his grave with the Judaizers in firm control of attitudes toward circumcision in Palestine. As remarked above, this controversy was finally settled by history rather than by negotiations when the Jewish insurrection of AD 66–73 was crushed by Rome, destroying the Temple and driving the religious leadership into exile. While that insight is both true and important, it does not answer the prior question of why, when the showdown came, the Jewish Christians refused to fight beside their Jewish countrymen, but migrated from Jerusalem to free themselves from the theocratic ideals of their ancestral religion.[8] We cannot be sure that Paul influenced this decision, but at least he left behind a clear witness for whoever would heed it.

What this brief review of the biblical evidence tells us is that God has commissioned us to work on overcoming controversy whether it be in good times or bad, whether we are likely to succeed or fail, whether we have the leadership of the church for or against us, whether it takes one time or multiple times to make progress, whether the issue is settled in our lifetime or after our death. This is not a headstrong approach to overcoming controversy, erroneously attributed to Paul, but an utter reliance on God to do his work of reconciliation through us. Many church leaders avoid the challenge of conflict resolution among Christians like a plague by muttering, somewhat sarcastically, that it would

---

[8]Both Eusebius (*Eccl. Hist.* III.2-3) and Epiphanius (*Ad. Haer.* xxix.7) identified Pella in Perea, a Greek city of the Decapolis, as the place of refuge. On problems with the choice of Pella as an asylum see S. G. F. Brandon, *The Fall of Jerusalem and the Christian Church* (London: S.P.C.K., 1957) 168-73.)

take a miracle to get feuding folks together again. But if a miracle be defined as a supernatural act of God in our world, then the transformation of hostility into peace is nothing less than a miracle because the Bible describes precisely that as the quintessential work of God. All that I am pleading for here is not to give up without really trying but to claim the promise of Jesus, "For mortals it is impossible, but for God all things are possible" (Mt. 19:26).

4. *Plead with God*. Throughout this chapter I have sought to emphasize that I am not against controversy as such but only against the kind of bickering among Christians that builds walls of hostility dividing the unity of the church into competing camps. Because I have been forced to deal with the kind of controversy that is bad for the church, let me conclude this study by considering the kind of controversy that is good for the church.

The bedrock of the biblical teachings on controversy is a distinctive conception of God. No deity in the ancient world was more exalted yet more involved in the plight of his people. Far from being aloof or indifferent, God took seriously the waywardness of Israel. In a favorite metaphor, he hauled them into court and held them accountable, by "preferring charges" or rendering a bill of indictment (Isa. 3:13-14a; Jer. 2:9; 25:31). A key contention of Scripture is: "The Lord has an indictment against the inhabitants of the Land" (Mic. 6:2; cf. Hos. 4:1).

The prophets were earthly agents of God's controversy; attorneys, as it were, for the divine plaintiff. Behind their furious denunciations lay the conviction that God is iconoclastic, an idol smasher who demands uncompromising loyalty and obedience from his people. But this was not caused by the fact that their God had a bad disposition or an ugly temper. Instead, the Lord was willing to "plead" his case (Hos. 12:2-3), to "let us argue it out" (Isa. 1:18); he was even willing to be corrected or proven wrong! God's indictment was really a lament expressed in what Abraham Heschel called the pathos of the prophets.[9]

Jesus was the supreme prophetic controversialist of all time. The divine lament was heard in the "woes" of Matthew 23 which ended with the tears of verses 37-38. As the Gospel of John dramatized it, Jesus' entire earthly ministry was God's way of putting Israel on trial. No wonder John 14--16 presents the Holy Spirit as a "Paraclete" or legal defender who serves as Christ's advocate in the continuing controversy over his claims asserted in the Gospel (Jn. 16:8-11). If Christianity is based on Christ, then it is controversial to the core both in substance and in spirit.

Christian history inherited this biblical dynamic and, if anything, intensified it for reasons inherent in the faith. For one thing, discipleship meant "living Christ," but there were four portraits of him in the Gospels, allowing a great deal of variety in the characteristics to be emphasized. For another thing, the original message had to be applied in new situations as Christianity moved from Jewish to Hellenistic culture, leading to continuing debate over how this could best be done. For a third thing, new heresies arose within the church, advocating convictions that resulted in tension and even schism.

As if all of this were not enough, there was the never-ending struggle to maintain the integrity of the church, which

---

[9]Abraham J. Heschel, *The Prophets* (New York: Harper & Row, 1962) 221-78, 489-92.

came to a climax in the Protestant Reformation. Martin Luther was a controversialist, as had been John Hus before him. Only a pitched battle could break the shackles of ecclesiastical corruption and launch a church "reformed and ever reforming itself" before God. This ferment gave rise to the Protestant principle anticipated in 1 Peter 4:17: judgment begins with the household of God. We preach a Word that judges us first and most severely.

The Baptists arose as purifiers. Their forerunners were called "separatists," "nonconformists," and "dissenters," all names for radical controversialists. They challenged the religious establishment, the rights of the crown, and the whole Constantinian synthesis of a thousand years. For them, Scripture shattered tradition; the Holy Spirit broke new light; conscience defied both conformity and continuity. With this background, Baptists felt right at home in the American Revolution, our country's great controversy with the Old World. In fact, they were in the vanguard of those who fought for the inalienable right to be religiously different even if it meant persecution and imprisonment.

What we have surveyed in this chapter are some of the ingredients for a theology of controversy. Strange that we should have so much controversy over doctrine but no doctrine of controversy! The evidence suggests that controversy is inescapable because it is inherent in the nature of Christian faith as a divine critique of all human life, religion included. Controversy is God's disturbing sign that "we know in part" (1 Cor. 13:12), that we have not yet arrived (Phil. 3:12), that even our faith may be wrong (Mt. 16:23)! It is an exasperating reminder that we apprehend so little of reality and understand so little even of what we do apprehend. At its best, controversy is the struggle by which we grow, purge our dross, sift out our chaff, chip away our barnacles, and search for the Mystery behind our maddening differences.

But all controversy is not "at its best." The New Testament speaks of "stupid controversies" and "silly speculations" (1 Tim. 1:4; 6:4; 2 Tim. 2:23) that lead to envy, dissension, slander, and suspicion. How can we avoid the wrangling that breeds hostility? By seeking clarity rather than victory. By critiquing issues rather than attacking persons. By viewing sincere opponents at their best rather than at their worst. By engaging in persuasion rather than in coercion. By giving both oneself and one's opponents the right to change their mind. Most of all, by allowing God to have a controversy with us before we try to have a controversy with others.

Now for the personal plea promised at the outset of this chapter. I have spent my vocational lifetime ministering in a denominational tradition that stressed above all else the building of New Testament churches. As this book seeks to demonstrate, the dominant characteristic of early Christianity was its daring to be different, even to the point of moving beyond circumcision, Sabbath observance, and temple sacrifice, all bulwarks of the Jewish parental religion, sanctioned by Scripture and centuries of observance. They pioneered a faith independent of any governmental entity (Phil. 3:20). They welcomed not only Greeks but barbarians as well (Rom. 1:4). They conferred spiritual equality on women and slaves (Gal. 3:28). And they made these kinds of breathtaking changes, most with remarkably little internal resistance, because they were needed by their movement if it was to become a truly universal faith.

How different is that dynamic in today's church? It almost seems as if some are trying to see how many groups they can exclude rather than include. For example, there are those who would limit the church only to Calvinists, or to inerrantists, or to conservatives, while others would limit the church to those holding the opposing views. But this is no way to build a worldwide church, which was the litmus test for settling doctrinal disputes in the apostolic age (Acts 15:7-9, 12, 14-18). To be sure, some progress has been made toward inclusiveness, but it is so often only a rearguard action, such as in the abolition of slavery, the crusade for women's suffrage, and extending the struggle for civil rights to minority groups. The tiny house-churches of the New Testament were not afraid to be *ahead* of their time whereas the huge Christian denominations of our day seem so timid that they end up *behind* their time.

So I plead with those who claim a high view of Holy Scripture: be first rather than last to bring heaven to earth, as our Lord taught us to pray (Mt. 6:10), not in order to attract attention by being faddish, but because we have already seen in Jesus what God's future looks like and have his empowering assurance that we can live that future now, in advance as it were, in our kind of world, before the end comes for us all.